INJ[U]

IN AN AC[CI]DEN[T]?

TEN OF AMERICA'S LEADING PERSONAL INJURY ATTORNEYS SHARE THEIR WISDOM.

Donald Marcari
Richard E. Spalding

Rutherford Publishing House
PO Box 969
Ramseur, NC 27316
www.RutherfordPublishingHouse.com

Cover photo: Stephen Coburn/Bigstock.com

ISBN-10: 0692298614
ISBN-13: 978-0692298619

TABLE OF CONTENTS

ACKNOWLEDGEMENTS

We all want to thank our husbands and wives, fathers and mothers, and everybody who has played a role in shaping our lives and our attitudes.

To all the clients we've had the honor of working with, who shaped our understanding of the difficulty of this time for you and your families. It has been our privilege to serve each and every one of you.

INTRODUCTION

Contributing Author:

Richard Erin Spalding

Host & Founder – Business
Leader Spotlight Show

As the host for the Business Leader Spotlight Show, I have had the opportunity to interview leading experts in various fields. In today's connected society, most people turn to the internet to get the majority of their information. Unfortunately, it has become difficult to distinguish good information from bad, because everyone can share anything online, whether it is true or false. The Business Leader Spotlight Show's goal is to be a central place where you can get valuable, accurate information about the topics we cover in the show. We try to accomplish this by interviewing the best of the best - standouts in their respective areas of expertise.

When we decided to publish a book on personal injury, we set out to identify the legal leaders on that subject and interview them to get their insights on the major issues relating to personal injury accidents. Unfortunately, it's impossible to get all the information one would want to know in a twenty minute interview. Today, we have over 5,000 minutes of expert advice from the best legal minds in the area of personal injury and wrongful death.

Introduction

We wanted the best-of-the-best personal injury attorneys collaborating on this book, so we asked the best ten out of more than 250 personal injury attorneys we interviewed to share with you their insights into what you should know before you settle your accident claim. I personally believe that this is the most powerful and enlightening book ever written on the subject. It is not just one lawyer's insights on personal injury accidents, but ten of the top personal injury attorneys in the United States, from different regions of the country, sharing with you the fruit of their years of experience.

It is our hope that reading this book has two outcomes for you: first, that you understand the process and the pitfalls that can be part of any personal injury or wrongful death claim; and second, armed with this knowledge, you are able to proceed with your claim in a way that not only allows you to achieve your goals, but to come out of the process with a sense that you are ready to begin a new chapter of your life.

In our interviews, one thing became crystal clear: most people don't want to sue other people because they don't want to hurt them financially or feel that it's not the Christian thing to do. It's important to understand that personal injury attorneys look to insurance policies to pay for your damages. These policies have been paid for by the defendant as protection in the event that another person is harmed. The injured party has a right to receive the insurance money as compensation for his or her injuries that were caused by the defendant's negligence.

This is why insurance companies are always involved in the claims process. The problem is that most people who are involved in an accident don't realize that insurance companies have no incentive to be fair or to fully compensate you for your injuries. By its very nature, a personal injury claim is adversarial between the injured party and the insurance company.

Unfortunately, personal injury claims against an insurance company can be viewed as a David-and-Goliath situation. As Goliath, well-funded insurance companies have well-trained insurance adjusters, in-house council, attorneys they hire outside the company, and expert witnesses. Their purpose is to either to find ways to deny your claim or find ways to minimize their liability and pay you as little as possible. The only way for you, as David, to level the playing field and be compensated fairly for your injuries is to hire an attorney who specializes in personal injury law.

Personal injury attorneys specialize in this area of the law and deal with insurance companies and their adjusters every day; therefore, personal injury attorneys know the tactics used by these companies and their agents. They can keep you safe from making unknown blunders that could have a detrimental effect on your case. For example, in some states you must deal with contributory negligence, which means that if you are one-percent at fault for the accident, you cannot recover any damages. You might make an innocent statement to the insurance adjuster (one who is trained to ask leading questions) that could jeopardize your claim against the at-fault driver in an automobile accident.

You will discover that the claim process is fraught with hidden landmines. Throughout this book, the top personal injury attorneys in the country share their knowledge with you. You will learn what many of the landmines are and how to avoid them. The information contained in this book could mean the difference between getting $5,000 versus $100,000 for your injuries.

You will learn about:
- Why you should hire a personal injury lawyer
- What a personal injury lawyer does
- What the landmines that you can face in a personal injury case are
- What subrogation rights are and how they can affect your payout
- What can happen if the other driver doesn't have insurance
- Why accidents involving a truck are different from those involving an automobile
- And so much more.

In the larger scheme of things, a personal injury attorney plays a critical role in society. They force manufacturers to keep our products safer and make people take responsibility by making them accountable for their actions. Without personal injury attorneys, we would live in a far more dangerous society.

As we compiled this book, one thing became crystal clear about the personal lawyers included here: the amount of money they make from your injury is not their goal. They understand that this is a highly emotional time in your life, and they see their role as someone who can compassionately take you by the hand and guide you through the claims process in a way to best achieve your goals.

Richard E. Spalding
Host & Founder – Business Leader Spotlight Show

1

THE MANY HATS OF A PERSONAL INJURY ATTORNEY

by Donald Marcari, Esq.

Donald Marcari, Esq.
Marcari, Russotto, Spencer & Balaban
Chesapeake, Virginia

Don first gained national attention when his exploits as a young defense attorney with the U.S. Navy Judge Advocate General's (JAG) Corps became the basis for the motion picture "A Few Good Men."

Don has been fighting for seriously injured people throughout North Carolina since 1985, and Virginia since 1988, concentrating on plaintiff personal injury law and civil litigation.

Don is a highly recognized attorney who has tried more than 200 jury trials, including cases against Ford, Firestone, American Honda, Home Depot, and several national trucking companies. He represented clients whose cases became the foundation for a movie, The Paula Coughlin Story, and a book, The Mother of All Hooks - The Story of the US Navy's Tailhook Scandal.

Don believes that people injured by the negligence of others often suffer serious physical, psychological, and financial damage. It is almost impossible to receive fair compensation without the help of a knowledgeable, caring lawyer who is experienced in personal injury law. When people ask why he likes being a lawyer, he responds, "I get the opportunity to help somebody every day. What could be better than that?."

THE MANY HATS OF A PERSONAL INJURY ATTORNEY

Many people wonder what a personal injury attorney does that is different than other types of attorneys. I tell them I wear many different hats.

My first hat is "investigator," because I must first investigate the claim. I visit the accident scene to make sure I fully understand how the accident happened and the dynamics involved. I try to preserve the scene as it looked that day by taking pictures from different angles as well as taking accurate physical measurements. This is important because in two or three years, if the case goes to trial, the accident scene may have changed. I also locate and interview witnesses to determine what they saw, who was present, what may have been said, and to ascertain other important details of the accident as they remember them. Again, it is important to do this quickly, before witnesses begin to forget the finer details of the accident.

The second hat is "medical coordinator." My primary concern is my client's well-being. The only remedy the law can provide in a personal injury case is money, which is a poor substitute for one's health. I want to make sure my clients visit the appropriate doctors for their injuries. Many clients think that their injuries will heal on their own. Some may, some may not. For a client who has only visited a family doctor and received pain medication, I may suggest visiting an orthopedic doctor and get a possible referral to physical therapy. Depending on the injuries, I may also suggest that my client see a chiropractor. Furthermore, I want to make sure that I receive copies of all medical records, so I can review those records as the case progresses. It's amazing how inaccurate these records can be and I want to get any mistakes corrected as quickly as possible.

The third hat is "negotiator." Once I have gathered all of the documents (pictures, medical bills and records, proof of lost wages, evidence of out-of-pocket expenses, etc.), I send out a settlement demand and begin negotiating with the insurance company. This part of my job also includes negotiating with health insurance companies to reduce any possible subrogation claims (which I will explain in greater detail later), so I can keep more money in my client's pocket. I might also need to negotiate with the medical providers and ask for reductions in any outstanding bills, all in an attempt to reduce the amount of money that must be paid to others out of the settlement proceeds.

The last hat, and the one that most people think of first, would be "litigator." Even though 85% of the cases settle prior to going to trial, the insurance company has to know that you are willing to go to court and will do a good job when you get there. Every case should be prepared from the beginning as if you were going to trial so, if you get to court, you can properly represent your client before a jury.

WATCH OUT FOR THESE LANDMINES

As far as "landmines" in personal injury cases, my firm faces several on a daily basis. The first landmine occurs when a client gives a statement to the insurance company, usually before he hires an attorney. At all times, clients must be truthful; at the same time, they should be aware that one statement, taken out of context or said in the wrong way, could end their claim before it begins. For example, immediately following an accident, the injured party may be on medication and may not even be sure what happened. If the insurance company calls the client for a statement, and the client is unsure as to what actually occurred or the sequence of events, speculating on details such as the speed of the other vehicle, the distances between the vehicles or other events could hurt the claim. Some states adhere to the doctrine of Contributory Negligence, which means that any negligence on the part of the injured party, often defined as being "1%" at fault, can bar him or her from recovering damages. An innocent statement such as, "Well, I was just driving down the road and I didn't see the oncoming car, and it hit me," can bar a claim against the other driver and his insurance company. The insurance company is recording every word; they can and will use any misstatement as evidence against the client to deny the claim.

At the outset of the case, the client should be extremely careful about what he says and to whom he says it. I often warn clients to be careful about what they say to their own doctors. There again, the client must be truthful; but be aware when you make a statement to your doctor, what you say is often written down in the medical records. Attorneys need accurate medical records which reflect the client's injuries both during negotiations, and especially when presenting evidence to a jury. I am often surprised what is written in the medical records. When I question my clients about these dubious statements, I frequently hear, "I didn't mean it that way," or, "I never said that." Clients must be specific because a doctor may dictate his notes later in the day or week when memories have faded. If a client is unsure about a detail or an event, he or she should not speculate. To avoid this landmine, clients should think about what they want to say and make sure their doctors understand their meaning precisely. Talking with an attorney first can help the client avoid these landmines.

Another landmine to avoid is signing documents in which you are uncertain as to their legal meaning and effect. Typically, clients will be presented with various forms at the doctor's office after an accident and will sign them without reading the fine print. These forms may state that the client gives the doctor the right to collect the client's insurance proceeds and assign other important rights over to the medical provider's office. The insurance company may also send the client forms that give them the right to collect the client's past medical history, get information regarding work history, or even limiting or relinquishing the right to pursue a claim by releasing the insurance company of any liability for some small payment of money. I constantly hear horror stories about clients who have signed such a "release" and now need additional medical care.

One of my clients who had been involved in a rear-end car collision and didn't think he was seriously injured, signed such a release accepting the insurance company's nominal settlement offer. He didn't want to "sue" anyone or make a big deal out of this "fender-bender." Unfortunately, he later realized that he had a herniated disc that required surgery. Since he had signed this release before knowing the full extent of his injuries the insurance company refused to pay. It took many years of litigation before he was finally able to get the compensation he deserved. Clients need to be aware of their rights and understand what they are signing so they can be treated fairly.

Social media has added yet another landmine to the practice of personal injury law, especially with the younger generation. Today, it seems everyone is connected through Facebook, Twitter, and YouTube, etc.; you can contact anyone, anywhere, anytime. As an attorney, I find it challenging when clients post information online that may be detrimental to their case. I explain to my clients that whatever they post online (no matter how private) is being exposed to the entire virtual world to see. Insurance companies are now able to request copies of the plaintiff's social media pages. Even the simplest posts can be taken out of context. In one case, my client alleged that she could not use her right arm effectively; however, she posted a picture of herself accepting a diploma and shaking the school president's hand. Needless to say, we had some very interesting discussions with the insurance company's attorney about that post. Clients need to be careful about what they post on social media regarding their accident and the effects it's had on them. I advise my clients that this is a personal matter that involves you, me, and the insurance company: we do not need to tell anyone else anything, unless the person is directly involved with the case. I caution my clients that whatever they want to say and post online is their decision, but the insurance company may be able to use that information against them. Insurance companies are always looking for a way to deflect blame away from their insured. You do not want to give them any more ammunition than necessary.

Some attorneys cause their own landmine by failing to adequately prepare their client for important events that arise in the case. For instance, the client's deposition which is when the insurance company's attorney gets to question the client about how the accident happened, his past medical history, how the accident has affected him, etc. At the deposition, the insurance company's attorney is trying to lock in the client's version of the events, evaluating the client as a witness, and determining if the jury will like the client. Before facing this pressure, it is best for the client to be fully prepared and to answer the questions asked accurately and honestly. If the client is unsure about an event then he needs to state that. It's never good to speculate or guess. Juries are human. They come into the courtroom not knowing anything about the client or the case. In a criminal case, the defendant is presumed innocent until proven guilty, even though it is often the other way around in real life. In a civil case, many jurors initially look at the plaintiff—the injured party—with skepticism. In my opinion, the insurance companies have done a good public relations job of implying that, "Anybody who sues is just after money and is greedy." In the courtroom, the biggest asset that the lawyer and the client have in their favor is credibility. So at the deposition, the insurance company attorney will be asking himself, "Is that somebody that the jury will like/relate to?" If the jury has empathy with the client, it will tend to be fairer in its verdict. On the other hand, if the client gets aggravated, confused, or frustrated while testifying, the jury may dislike or not believe him.

Attorneys should not wait to prepare their client for a deposition until the day of the deposition, or worse, thirty minutes before it begins. Attorneys need to meet with their client a day or two before the deposition so the client is properly prepared to answer the questions truthfully, and to refrain from answering questions if he is unsure of the answer. Given that it may be two or three years after the event in question, it is perfectly acceptable if the client does not remember every detail clearly. If that is the case, the appropriate answer is, "I do not remember." To ensure the accuracy of each statement, clients should take the time to think about each question and respond appropriately.

I encourage my clients to dress appropriately for depositions; business casual is the preferred mode of dress. They should also be well-rested beforehand. This testimony given by the client is crucial: the deposition is not just a "check the box" process. Many times, it is the deciding factor in whether the client's case will settle or proceed to court. Frequently after a "good" deposition I have been approached by the insurance attorney in the hallway and told, "We should be able to settle this, I'll see if I can get you some more money." This possibility makes it imperative that the client be prepared for the deposition.

PEOPLE JUST WANT TO BE TREATED FAIRLY

By its very nature, a personal injury claim is adversarial. Even after being involved in an accident that is not your fault and being injured, most people don't want to file a claim or get involved in the litigation process; most just want to be treated fairly. When a potential client asks me why he should hire a personal injury attorney, I point out one very important thing: insurance companies have experts on their side, so should you. Insurance companies have a vast team:

adjusters trained to handle claims, in-house counsel, outside attorneys, and expert witnesses. You need someone on your side that is as equally well-equipped.

Insurance companies are in businesses to make money; they have no incentive to be fair. With their business model they have to take in more in premium dollars than they pay out in claims. The bigger the difference, the better their balance sheet looks. They evaluate their adjusters on how they handle their claims, thus giving adjusters an incentive to close that claim as quickly as possible, paying as little as possible, getting the release signed, and moving on to the next claim. I am not suggesting that insurance adjusters are bad people: many adjusters are very good people. Conversely, I do not think that anyone I have represented is trying to scam the system: my clients simply want full and fair compensation for what they lost and what they are having to endure due to someone else's carelessness. The interest of each party is different.

As an attorney, my job is to review the case and determine what is fair in the eyes of the law, while also helping the insurance adjuster to see and understand how this injury has affected my client's life. I want to get to personally know each of my clients so I will have an advantage over the insurance adjuster in negotiations. I can better advocate for my client by demonstrating to the adjuster what my client has been through and what he will continue to face due to the negligence of their insured. By knowing my client better, I can convincingly show the insurance company what is fair and why it is fair, based on the facts of the case. We are taught responsibility by our parents, role models, and teachers from the time we enter grade school - if we cause harm, we should be held responsible. On behalf of my client, I just want the negligent party to be responsible for all the damage they have caused.

Unfortunately, in personal injury cases, the only remedy the law can provide the injured party is money. This tends to cheapen the process, because money cannot restore the client's health, which is the most important thing. For those that are seriously injured, it can help pay for future medical expenses and other necessities that will help make the clients' life a little easier, but the vast majority of seriously injured clients I have represented would prefer not to have been involved in such a life altering event.

One case that comes to mind involved a gentleman (I will call him "Bob") who was almost sixty-five years old—two weeks away from retirement—when he was injured. Bob had worked hard all his adult life as a commercial fisherman. He was in excellent physical condition; he could pick up more than 200 crab pots per day. As he was driving his car one Saturday afternoon, a big company truck crossed the centerline, crashing into his car head-on. Bob was in the hospital for a month due to his injuries. He lost one of his eyes and fractured his hip, along with several ribs. The prognosis was that he would never be able to walk again. My firm filed a lawsuit and proceeded to court-ordered mediation.

The case did not settle during the first mediation, which is typical in big cases. During the second mediation, we were able to settle the case for an amount in the seven-figures. Bob told me, "Tell that company they can keep their money. I just want my health back." My firm worked very hard to ensure that the money Bob received would make his life easier. We helped Bob find a handicap-accessible van and a home with handicap ramps. We also set up an annuity so that Bob would have a steady stream of income for the remainder of his life. Everything was done to make Bob's life as easy as possible, but the money really didn't compensate Bob for the injuries he sustained in the accident.

Experienced personal injury attorneys can maximize the recovery for their clients by making sure the insurance company has evidence regarding all the elements of damages which can be awarded. For example, compensation for pain and suffering, reimbursement for the medical bills incurred and any future medical bills, lost wages, lost earning capacity, permanent disfigurement, or loss of function. An attorney has to differentiate which of these damages are quantifiable and which are subjective—such as pain and suffering—and try to place a realistic value on that element of damages.

Physical pain and mental suffering are an important part of the damages in any personal injury claim, but it is often difficult for juries to award money for them. Some jurors think that money can't make the pain go away or that, since you can't quantify it, it is just too difficult to award money for pain and suffering. When speaking to potential jurors I ask them, "Since you cannot see pain or you cannot measure pain, will you still consider that an element of damages that you will consider in your verdict?" I try to get them to relate it to something in their everyday life. For instance, is it worth $5.00 a day, what they paid for parking, or something more? I also try to get them thinking about other aspects of everyday life that this accident has affected. If my client had an older car that was paid for and in good mechanical condition but now has to buy another car, or if he is having trouble getting to work or taking his kids to school, how does that affect someone? What if my client cannot coach Little

League anymore or his wife has to take over cutting the lawn or someone needs to take a pain reliever every day. Each of those situations shows the client suffers now because of injuries sustained in the accident. I relay all these experiences to the adjuster and/or to the jury for their consideration.

Many times the attorney and the insurance adjuster don't agree. When there is a difference of opinion as to the value of the case I must be ready, willing, and able to take the case to court on behalf of my client. If I am not willing to do so, my client may not receive full and fair compensation for the claim. If an attorney is not willing to go to court, then he should not take the case in the beginning. I have received referrals from other attorneys who originally thought that the personal injury case they agreed to take would be "easy" and would settle quickly for a fair amount. Once involved they realized that there are many complex elements to handling a personal injury case. Attorneys must evaluate the strengths and weaknesses in determining liability while also reviewing all the elements of the damages. Handling a personal injury case isn't easy.

After twenty-eight years of handling cases, I can tell you that there is no book to go to which will tell you what a case is worth or what constitutes full and fair compensation. An attorney who practices this type of law deals daily with insurance adjusters and/or their attorneys, so he knows the tactics used by these companies to minimize the value of the case.

HIRE AN EXPERIENCED PERSONAL INJURY ATTORNEY AS SOON AS POSSIBLE

It is extremely important to hire an experienced attorney as soon as possible after a catastrophic injury. The client needs an attorney who has experience in dealing with this type of injury, because the process is very complex. Expert witnesses may be needed to adequately demonstrate the extent of the client's damages. For example, an economist can show the monetary losses incurred due to the lost earning capacity of the client for the remainder of his life. If the client is able to return to work in some capacity, a vocational rehabilitation expert can help the patient find a new career path and show the difference in wages. Many people do not want to just sit at home, so it's necessary to determine what work they can do given their education, experience, and now-limited physical condition.

With catastrophic events such as wrongful death, severe injuries such as brain damage, or botched surgeries, the first area of concern is the amount of insurance coverage available. Some states only require automobile coverage as low as $15,000. I always advise my clients to look at their own insurance policies and to protect themselves by carrying uninsured/underinsured motorist coverage or even umbrella coverage. These types of insurance coverage are fairly inexpensive and are a good investment to protect yourself and your family, as there are many people driving on our roadways with minimum or no insurance coverage at all due to the tough economic times.

Medical bills alone can quickly climb into thousands of dollars with any one of these examples: hospital stays, surgeries, MRIs, CAT scans, or other diagnostic tests. If there is not enough insurance to cover the anticipated total of the medical bills, an attorney may want to quickly settle the case for the available policy limits, to prevent all of the settlement money from going to the medical providers. The attorney can then help the client determine alternative ways to pay for the medical expenses such as Medicare, Medicaid, or the client's own health insurance.

After checking the insurance coverage, an attorney should also perform an asset check on the defendant to determine if he or she has any assets to add to the insurance coverage or that can pay any excess of the jury verdict.

It's always challenging to find ways to explain the extent of the client's injuries to the jury. I recently met with a high-wage earning client who was involved in a serious accident in which she sustained a mild traumatic brain injury. She initially thought, "Why do I need an attorney? It should be self-evident that the insurance company needs to reimburse me for my losses." Unfortunately, the system does not work like that. Before beginning to think about a settlement, a lot of information must be gathered particularly regarding the extent of the injuries sustained. Our brain is an amazing organ that controls so much of our bodily functions. It is like jelly sitting inside our skull which is filled with ridges and sharp points. The brain can be easily injured in an accident; a direct blow doesn't need to be sustained. Brain injuries may take years to heal, or may not heal at all. Attorneys must begin by asking the client, or even family members, questions such as, "Does light bother you?" and "Are you forgetting things?" Sometimes, the injured party doesn't even realize that he has suffered a brain injury until his attorney begins asking friends and family members if they have noticed anything different about the client after the accident, such as a sensitivity to light or sound, changes in personality, such as a new tendency to get easily frustrated, angry, or to forget things.

An attorney who has determined that his client has suffered a brain injury must proceed with getting the proper diagnosis and employing the appropriate experts. It may be necessary for the client to complete neuropsychological testing. Some clients question why they need this testing if they have already been examined by a neurologist or neurosurgeon. Neuropsychological testing actually shows what areas of the brain have been affected and the extent of the damage due to the accident. These deficits can then be explained to the jury.

Pictures and medical illustrations are a dramatic way of making your point to the adjuster or the jury. One of my clients was seriously injured from head to toe. For his case, I presented a life-sized, six-foot medical illustration that showed each of his injuries, beginning at the top of his head, all the way down to his toes. The medical illustration was very graphic and actually showed his face, so that the jury could relate to the injuries. With the illustration, I could explain to the jury each part of the body that was injured.

In the past, it seemed an attorney only needed to negotiate with the at-fault person's insurance company to settle a claim. Today, the attorney is forced to negotiate with many different entities and insurance companies, including the client's own health insurance company. Many health insurance companies today are asserting their "subrogation rights," or the right of the health insurance company to be reimbursed from the client's settlement proceeds for the monies they spent paying for the client's medical expenses. Many states have anti-subrogation statutes which prevent this. However, under a federal statute, the Employee Retirement Income Security Act (ERISA), this is now being allowed. Some health insurance companies are going so far as to not paying the medical bills until the client signs an agreement allowing the health insurance company to be fully reimbursed, thereby leaving the client with nothing. This has to be addressed at the beginning of the case by telling the health insurance company you are not going to pursue a claim unless there is some compromise. Attorneys also negotiate with medical care providers who don't want to submit the bills to Medicare, etc., due to the low reimbursement rates. The attorney may also have to deal with the client's own automobile insurance company, in addition to the defendant's insurance company, depending on the type of coverage under the client's policy.

One of my current cases involves a client who was struck from behind by a car and seriously injured while riding on a bicycle. His medical bills alone are over $50,000; however, there is only $100,000 worth of car insurance coverage available to him. His health insurance company is refusing to pay the medical expenses unless he signs a subrogation agreement. If he does sign this agreement, he will likely get nothing from the settlement. If he does not sign the agreement, his health insurance company will not pay the medical bills; the medical providers will turn the bills over to collections, and his credit will be ruined. Rather than allow this to happen, I contacted the health insurance company to discuss our options. I explained to the company that it does not make any sense for my client to take time off from work and to incur expenses from a lawsuit, simply to win money for the health insurance company. It would make more sense for him not to pursue the claim than go through the stress and expense of a lawsuit for the benefit of the health insurance company. Rather than advising him to take this course, we agreed to work with the health insurance company to negotiate a repayment that will compensate my client, while giving some money back to the insurance company.

These situations are becoming more common with regard to subrogation claims and agreements, and need to be treated with great care. Individuals are signing these agreements without fully understanding what they are signing; they certainly don't understand that they are giving up their rights to the health insurance company.

As an attorney, I try to stay ahead of any issues and deal with them right from the beginning of the case. I examine my client's health insurance policy to see if it qualifies under ERISA and has valid subrogation rights. If so, I must determine how to handle the reimbursement provisions set forth in the plan. By dealing with subrogation rights at the beginning of a case, I will have more bargaining power than if I wait until the end of the case when the insurance company is there to collect the money, and my client is left with nothing. I investigate the defendant's insurance coverage and look for other available insurance coverage, including my client's own automobile coverage. I advise my clients to use their health insurance coverage to pay medical bills; at the end of the case, any unpaid medical bills must be paid out of the settlement proceeds. My goal is to help my clients return to their normal lives, or live a life that is as close as possible to the one they had before the accident occurred.

THE CHANGING POLITICAL CLIMATE CAN IMPACT YOUR CASE

I have had to deal with many changes in handling personal injury cases during my twenty-eight years of practicing law, including the changing political climate. Each year, it seems it is more difficult to handle personal injury cases: maybe it's because the insurance companies have such a powerful lobby in Washington, DC and in our states' capitals. Laws are being passed which limit the insurance companies' responsibility to pay a full and fair amount of compensation to the injured party.

In one state where I practice, a law called "Bill Versus Paid" was recently enacted. According to this law, the injured party can only offer into evidence the remaining amount owed on the medical bills, rather than the full cost of the medical treatment for the injuries sustained in the accident. For patients who have private health insurance or have Medicare and Medicaid, there is often a substantial write-off from the original amount of the bill. The result is that the amount of the actual bill allowed into evidence is minimal, compared to the actual cost of treatment. Even though patients may have serious injuries, the medical bills that are considered as "evidence" do not fairly reflect the injuries sustained by the person.

I have also seen insurance companies working very hard to limit the amount of money that can legally be paid for a claim by placing a cap on the amount of damages that can be awarded. Let's imagine for a moment that your child has suffered a brain injury and needs a life care plan because he will need constant attention for the rest of his life: maybe another sixty or seventy years. In some states, the cap on a jury award is $2 million. No matter what the jury decides, the judge has to reduce the verdict down to $2 million. Once the attorney's fees, the costs of litigation, and payment towards the substantial medical bills are subtracted, very little money remains for this child and his family.

In my opinion, it is ridiculous that we allow a jury to decide if someone should live or die in the criminal system, without having enough confidence in that same jury to award a fair amount of compensation for someone's injury. In the civil justice system I do not understand how a right-minded person can believe that caps on a jury award are fair.

MOTORCYCLE CASES

I would now like to take a moment to explore two different kinds of injury cases: those involving motorcycles and large trucks. I used to be an avid motorcyclist, but I've since realized this amazing truth: automobile drivers don't seem to be able to see motorcycle riders. As a biker, I have experienced that moment of disbelief when a car merges into my lane as though my motorcycle and I were invisible. The truth is motorcycle accidents are generally true tragedies. When a motorcyclist is hit by a 6,000-pound vehicle, he or she inevitably sustains serious injuries. Because of this, attorneys handling these cases must carefully investigate all sources of available insurance coverage.

In a motorcycle case, it is important for the client to keep the motorcycle as evidence. If at all possible, the client should not allow the insurance company to take the motorcycle. If a lawsuit needs to be filed and the case proceeds to trial, the motorcycle is a graphic illustration for the jury's benefit of the damages sustained. Additionally, there could be a product liability claim to pursue.

Another important aspect of a motorcycle accident case is ensuring that the client sees the appropriate doctors. Since broken bones are common, the client should see an orthopedic doctor. Road rash and scarring is another big problem in these cases even when the rider is wearing leather clothing and a helmet. The client will need to see a plastic surgeon, though the surgeon will usually want to wait approximately a year after the accident to see how the scars are healing.

The perception of motorcyclists is another difficult aspect of these cases. While many people own and ride motorcycles (including professionals such as myself), some people have preconceived notions about motorcyclists and assume that the plaintiff got what he deserves. Attorneys must address this from the very beginning with the jury, and question the prospective jurors to weed out any jurors with such beliefs. I prepare my clients for this possible roadblock by telling them to be themselves in the courtroom. If they have tattoos or long hair, fine: let's talk about that and be comfortable when we go into court. If people are open and honest in the courtroom, the jury will begin to realize that the plaintiff is a person just like them, with the same wants and desires that they themselves experience. Prejudices are hard to overcome, but they must be addressed up front: do not act as if they do not exist.

TRUCK ACCIDENTS REQUIRE SPECIAL HANDLING

Trucking accident cases are also handled somewhat differently than regular automobile accident cases. Given the disparity between the vehicles, someone is usually seriously injured. The most important thing to do in a truck accident case is to get to the scene of the accident as quickly as possible. The trucking company and its insurance carrier usually have safety teams that will be at the scene before the trucks or vehicles are moved. It is amazing how quickly these teams can get to the scene of an accident. Since they will be taking measurements and gathering evidence, a representative of the injured party must also get there quickly to conduct his own investigation.

A "spoliation letter" must immediately be sent to the trucking company and the insurance carrier, advising them not to destroy or erase the information contained on the truck's black box and other important information. The data on this black box contains important information about what the truck was doing just prior to the accident, such as how fast it was traveling and if the brakes were applied. The victim's representative must obtain that evidence from the black box before it can be destroyed or erased. You would hate to think that anyone would destroy evidence: however, it's better to be safe.

Every person or company involved should be put on notice: the trailer owner, the tractor owner, the driver, and every insurance company involved. The discovery requests in trucking accident cases also differ from any other type of personal injury case, because of the amount of data involved in a trucking accident. For example, truck drivers are only allowed to drive for a certain number of hours; these hours are carefully logged. Copies of the logs for the driver and the logs for the truck should be obtained, to help determine if the trucker was driving more hours than allowed. The logs will also reveal where the driver has been, where he was going, what load he was carrying, and what stops he made along the way. A thorough investigation must be done in a truck accident case, as early as possible.

DON'T WAIT – REVIEW YOUR PERSONAL AUTOMOBILE POLICY TODAY

I would advise everyone to take a good look at his or her own automobile insurance policy to determine what types of coverage he or she has and the amount. Most people do not know as much about their own insurance coverage as they should: they simply meet with an insurance agent, who sells them a policy so that they can drive. They usually tell their insurance agent, "Give me the cheapest policy that you can." In these tough times, many people find it difficult to put food on the table, pay rent, and cover basic living expenses; insurance coverage is the last thing on their minds. However, it is important to keep in mind that good insurance coverage is not simply a necessary evil, it's vital in today's world.

Why do I say that? Many people are driving without any insurance coverage or they are only covered by the state minimum. Depending on the state, minimum coverage can be as low as $10,000 to $15,000. Clients should carefully review their insurance policies to determine what coverage is available to them, beginning with liability coverage. What if the client caused the accident, and has only $25,000 in liability insurance coverage? If the case is worth $50,000, the client may personally face exposure for that extra $25,000. The client does not want to be sued for something that was an accident. However, without sufficient liability insurance coverage, the client could be forced into bankruptcy. Therefore, everyone should have liability coverage of at least $100,000.

The next area to review is that of uninsured or underinsured coverage. Uninsured coverage protects clients if someone causes an accident and does not have insurance; underinsured coverage protects clients if someone only has the state's minimum insurance limits. Uninsured and underinsured coverages are optional (clients must choose to add these to their existing policies), but the cost is relatively inexpensive compared to the benefits. There again, I would strongly recommend at least $100,000 in coverage.

When the other driver is uninsured or underinsured, clients can go against their own insurance companies to collect damages for their injuries if they have the above-mentioned coverages. Since they will now be in an adversarial position against their own insurance companies, they should not assume that their insurance companies will willingly write a check simply because the clients have always paid their premiums on time. The client may need an attorney to ensure that his or her rights are protected, even against his or her own insurance company.

Another type of automobile insurance coverage that is important is called "Medical payments coverage." As with underinsured and uninsured coverage, clients have the opportunity to inexpensively protect themselves. Medical payment coverage can be purchased in increments starting at $1,000; this coverage will pay for accident-related medical bills—including the medical bills of any passengers in the accident—regardless of fault. This can be particularly important for people who are not covered by health insurance.

Finally, an umbrella policy is important when someone has personal assets to protect. Umbrella policies of $1 million and $2 million are still relatively inexpensive, but offer a great amount of protection, especially since medical expenses can quickly add up in a serious accident. Clients should make sure that their umbrella policy also covers uninsured and under-insured motorists. With the number of people texting and driving these days, it is worthwhile for clients to check their policies and add additional coverage to protect them in the event of an accident.

I represented a nineteen-year-old newlywed, who was seriously injured in a car accident; her husband was in the military. A trailer came loose from a truck traveling in the opposite direction on the interstate, crossed the median, and struck my client's vehicle head-on. She was uninjured from the neck down, but was hospitalized for a month with a very serious brain injury. Due to the severity of her brain injury, she could not be left alone and required constant care. Her husband had to leave the military so that he could stay home and care for his wife. My firm checked the insurance coverage for the driver, the truck owner, and the trailer owner (all owned by different people), and we were able to get her a substantial recovery. However, in this case, the victim's life expectancy was another fifty to sixty years, and she would require constant care during that time. Even though we were able to put money in a trust and the husband was able to purchase a handicap-accessible home, he had to leave the military so he could stay home with his wife and care for her. Thankfully in this case, there was sufficient insurance coverage; if the owners had only carried minimum coverage, it could have been more devastating.

WHAT TO LOOK FOR WHEN HIRING AN ATTORNEY

The sooner the victim hires a competent attorney, the better off he or she will be. Many things change quickly with personal injury cases. Witnesses move, memories fade, and accident scenes change. If proper medical treatment is not sought, that may be used against you. The client may be asked to sign releases or may be coerced into saying something detrimental to the case. The longer the injured party waits, the greater the damage could be to the case and the less compensation could be received. Some people think, "I will wait to see what the insurance company will offer me before calling an attorney." During that time, the insurance companies will have set their reserves which may restrict the voluntary potential pay out on the claim.

It does not cost anything to meet with an attorney to discuss a claim and the rights of the injured party. Most personal injury attorneys work on a contingency-fee basis, which means that clients do not pay any attorneys' fees until and unless they receive a settlement or verdict. Attorneys in other areas of law charge by the hour, and clients usually have to pay a retainer fee: however, most personal injury attorneys are paid a flat percentage at the end of the case. They work hard for their clients from the moment the client walks into the office.

Many attorneys advertise on television, websites, and bill-boards, etc. You need to investigate the person you are going to hire to represent you. In a personal injury case, you can do several things to make sure that you are hiring the right attorney for you:

First, look for someone who concentrates his or her practice on personal injury law. With today's complex and ever-changing laws, it is difficult for an attorney to be experienced in all areas of law. It is better to focus on the area where experience is most needed.

Second, ask for attorney recommendations from friends, family, and other people that you trust. You want an attorney who is a strong advocate, willing to go "all out" to protect your interests. Attorneys cannot guarantee results; however, you want to know that your attorney is going to give your case his or her best effort.

Third, call the attorney and talk on the telephone. No attorney should be afraid to answer any questions that you may have about personal injury cases in general, or your own case in particular. Ask the attorney questions such as, "How many cases have you handled?" and, "Are you willing to go to court?" Attorneys do not have a crystal ball and every case is different, but the least they can offer you is examples from their own past experiences.

Fourth and most importantly, find someone with whom you are very comfortable. You will be sharing a lot of important aspects of your life with this person. Since your prior medical history and even your finances could come into play during the case, you need someone that you can confide in and trust.

The best advice that I can give to anyone involved in an accident is the same advice that I would give to a member of my family: hire a competent attorney who concentrates in the area of personal injury. If you were buying a home or preparing a will, I would tell you to find an attorney that is competent in those areas of law. The biggest problem I see is when people believe they can handle a claim on their own. The insurance company will advise the injured person against hiring a lawyer, under the excuse that lawyers will take one-third of the settlement from the injured party. On the contrary, studies have shown that an injured person who hires a competent attorney receives four times the amount of compensation, compared to someone who represents himself. Accident victims should hire an attorney who is honest and competent; a strong advocate with whom the victim will feel comfortable and who will fight for the victim's rights.

(This content should be used for informational purposes only. It does not create an attorney-client relationship with any reader and should not be construed as legal advice. If you need legal advice, please contact an attorney in your community who can assess the specifics of your situation.)

2

SHOULD YOU GO IT ALONE OR HIRE A QUALIFIED PERSONAL INJURY ATTORNEY?

by Douglas R. Zanes, Esq.

Douglas R. Zanes, Esq.

Zanes Law
Tucson and Phoenix, Arizona

Doug Zanes is a no-nonsense attorney with a soft side. He entered into personal injury law to bring justice to those in need. "Bad accidents happen and there's nothing anyone can do to change that," he says. "I take pride in the fact that we are willing to start that fight for our clients so that they are completely compensated, and we are willing to take that fight to the end for them."

"We're not like most law firms. Our clients are family to us. We're never too busy to assist them and their families, long after their cases are done."

Zanes Law has represented thousands of clients and recovered tens of millions of dollars. He is a member of the Million Dollar Advocates Forum – less than 1% of U.S. lawyers are admitted to this group, which is limited to those who have won settlements exceeding $1 million.

SHOULD YOU GO IT ALONE OR HIRE A QUALIFIED PERSONAL INJURY ATTORNEY?

So I believe one of the first things that must be addressed when discussing personal injury cases is a question that may be on some potential clients' minds: "Why should I hire an attorney and pay him a third of my recovery?" The common sentiment in this case being: "If I do it on my own and can obtain the same resolution as an attorney would, then I'll come away with more money in my pocket." I typically charge a contingency fee for representing most personal injury clients, which means that I am only paid if I obtain a settlement for my client. A contingency fee of one-third seems to be the standard industry rate for most personal injury cases. In other words, if I obtain a $90,000 settlement, my attorney fee will be $30,000 (one-third of the settlement amount). However, some attorneys charge either a bit more or a bit less than this percentage.

Unfortunately, injury victims often think in terms of making money on their case when they decide to forego representation. They assume that if they can settle their case for $10,000, then they have essentially just made $3,300 by declining to hire a personal injury attorney. The problem that individuals with this thought pattern encounter is that the personal injury claims process is much more complicated today than it was fifteen to twenty years ago. Insurance companies no longer simply settle cases, but rather, choose to aggressively defend and fight personal injury cases. Historically, even ten to fifteen years ago, insurance companies had a much different approach: they settled more claims and fought fewer cases. Individuals who have never been through a personal injury case are simply not equipped to counter the tactics insurance companies use to defend claims these days. Because of this it is extremely difficult for someone who is not a personal injury attorney to obtain that full value offer, and it is also extremely difficult for them to actually know what the real value of their claim is.

Today, an insurance company's perspective is: "This is a business and from a business perspective, the less money we pay out in claims, the more profit we make." For this reason, they fight both small and large claims indiscriminately, because they employ a business approach that is meant to increase their profits. I'm not certain that potential clients truly understand this concept when they begin the claims process. Of course, many people see only the familiar television commercials featuring insurance companies. These advertisements, which are designed to gain the trust of potential buyers, are simply a marketing strategy they use to bring in more business and to make more money. Nevertheless, they give the impression that the insurance company is there to protect you, whether to help you when you are injured by one of their insured customers, or to protect you if you carry their insurance policy and injure another party. This is just not the case—the goal of the insurance company is not to protect customers, but to pay out as little as possible in claims, which also helps their bottom line.

I really believe that people who have been injured benefit greatly from the experience of a personal injury attorney precisely because he or she handles such cases on a daily basis. An attorney understands the complexity of the process, and knows how to handle an insurance company determined to fight your claim. Rather than proceeding in a straightforward manner, there will always be a counter-argument to deal with when bringing a personal injury claim. The insurance company will say, "Well, we disagree with you. We don't think that your client was hit that hard because we have estimated the cost to repair the client's vehicle at $1,500." Then, the insurance company will continue to argue that the part being replaced had minimal damage, which indicates that the client could not possibly have sustained the types of injuries being claimed. They are therefore unwilling to pay the amount being claimed by the injured party.

This type of counter-argument, a typical part of the process, is what makes dealing with personal injury claims so much more complicated than the average person hoping to "go it alone" anticipates. My perspective has always been that he who has the check, has the power to decide whether or not to write that check. The only advantage that our clients have in any case is their ability to file a lawsuit if they disagree with the insurance company's handling of the claim. Insurance companies also know that they are not in danger of being sued by someone who has not retained an attorney. They have handled insurance claims for decades, basically ever since vehicles and insurance came into existence, and process tens of thousands of claims in a single year. They have an incredible amount of experience in dealing with claimants and have access to just about any resource they could need or want in order to defend a personal injury claim. Insurance companies will hire experts to support their position and retain any attorneys needed to fight against your claim. Therefore, the only advantage an individual who has been hurt in an accident by an at-fault individual has is the right to file a lawsuit.

In my experience, an insurance company will always offer a smaller settlement when you represent yourself because, quite simply, they will always pay less money when they are not afraid of a lawsuit. However, I also think you run into the same kind of problem if you happen to hire the wrong law firm. It is interesting because, unlike other areas of practice, many attorneys believe they have what it takes to defend a personal injury case. On the other hand, if someone is looking for a divorce attorney and he or she happens to call an attorney who does not practice family law, that attorney will simply refer the client to someone who does handle divorces. Unfortunately, most attorneys assume that car accident cases are easy money for their law firm and will often accept this type of case even though they have little to no experience with car accident claims and may never have tried a personal injury case before. I think when an individual hires an in-experienced attorney, he is in just as bad a position as if he had handled the case without representation.

Insurance companies spend thousands of dollars defending these types of claims and know just which attorneys handle these cases on a regular basis. They know which ones will sue them and take the case to a jury trial and which will settle the case to avoid a trial. Insurance companies thus treat attorneys and law firms differently based on this knowledge and on the track record of the attorney and his law firm. When we first began our law practice 11 years ago, we had to fight, fight, and fight on every case to build a reputation within the legal and insurance community of aggressively representing clients and being unafraid to take cases to trial when necessary. By doing so, we got good results, which turned into even better results as the years progressed. We typically resolve 90% of our personal injury cases for the amount that we want without having to file a lawsuit. We only file suit in about 10% of them, which I believe is the norm for these types of cases. However, it took a lot of work, dedication, and willingness to litigate many cases, for us to get to where we are today. Individuals who attempt to represent themselves do not have this kind of solid foundation and reputation to rely upon when going up against an insurance company.

I think anyone who has been injured in an accident or due to negligence of some kind should consider hiring an attorney to represent him or her, because in the end, my opinion is that he or she will be better off for it. Yes, you can represent yourself, but at what cost? If you have never handled a personal injury case, it will certainly take you a lot of time to hone the skills and knowledge of the law that you'll need in order to represent yourself. It will take much more effort and many more resources on your part to handle the case on your own. Hiring a personal injury attorney who handles such cases on a daily basis and who will almost always get you more money than you would have gotten on your own, even after deducting attorney fees, is a no-brainer. In fact, this is the thought process I use when I need something done myself.

I feel as though I am a pretty smart person. I can certainly read books about home repairs and buy the parts that I'll need at Home Depot in order to do a repair myself. But when a pipe breaks at my house, it will take me an inordinate amount of time and effort to first learn what I need to know to fix it and then to actually perform the task. Even if I do figure out how to repair the pipe, chances are, the end result will not be of the same quality as it would have been if I had just hired a professional. An experienced plumber can take care of this issue in an hour and do it correctly. For this service, I will gladly pay him, because it allows me to focus my efforts on things that I am more skilled in.

The same principle holds for my law firm. Even though I am an attorney, there are times when I need advice regarding leases or business issues. I do not simply say, "I am an attorney so I will just figure it out myself." Instead, I hire an attorney who specializes in lease agreements, business issues, estate planning, or other types of law; someone with expertise in these areas, to advise me on the issues that I need help with at that time. For instance, when I need assistance drawing up my attorney compensation agreements, I hire an employment law attorney to help ensure that my agreements are the way that they legally need to be. Years ago, I heard that only a fool represents himself. It's not as though I look at it precisely in that way, because I do think our clients are smart and could probably do it, if they applied themselves. I just think they are much better off when they allow us to represent them because we do it every day and handle thousands of cases. Any good personal injury attorney will give you that same benefit.

VALUING YOUR CLAIM

Another huge challenge that anyone attempting to handle his or her own personal injury case encounters is how to value the claim. There is no easy mathematical calculation that one can perform to produce a figure for the insurance company to pay. Years ago, when insurance companies were more willing to pay claims, tripling the medical costs seemed to be the "mathematical equation" that many attorneys and insurance companies relied upon to determine the value of the claim. Of course, this approach was only used in simple personal injury cases and rarely in cases that involved serious personal injury. Needless to say, this has no application for determining how a claim is valued today. I am not even sure where that concept originated, but the process of valuing a claim has become much more complicated in recent years. It is more an art than a science.

For instance, the value of a case can depend heavily on the city in which the accident occurred and the jurisdiction in which the lawsuit will be filed. When we assess a case, we ask ourselves, "If we put this case in front of either a jury or an arbitrator, what might the award be and why would it be that particular amount?" If I file a lawsuit and we end up in front of a jury in Pima County for an accident that occurred in Tucson, Arizona, the real determining factor for the case value is based on what we anticipate the jury might do with the claim. A jury in Tucson, Arizona will undoubtedly be different from a jury in Del Rio, Texas. One may be more or less conservative than the other with regard to the amount of an award. What attorneys bring to the table is their experience in understanding how a jury thinks. We have a very good idea as to what a jury will do depending on the nature of the case because we spend a good deal of time in front of juries. We also spend a significant amount of time researching jury verdicts to determine what plaintiffs are being paid for different types of injuries and damages in various jurisdictions.

At the end of last year, I was informed by one of my firm's attorneys that a Pima County Superior Court judge confirmed that our law firm had tried 13% of all civil cases tried in the county that year. This particular attorney had been involved in a third of the trials that had come before this judge during the course of that year. The percentage confirms that we have seen many trials and many cases. This is why we know the value of a claim; because we identify and evaluate which cases did and did not work out as anticipated. Again, individuals trying to represent themselves have absolutely no way of knowing this kind of information, so are unable to use it to their advantage in the way that we can. They've just not had the experience we have had in trying cases before a jury, which is why it is so beneficial to hire an experienced personal injury attorney rather than attempt to settle your claim on your own.

It is also possible to have two very different claim values for the same injury. Someone with a broken leg that requires surgery to insert plates, pins, and rods is going to have a much higher claim value than someone who suffers a more minor injury that has completely healed after visiting a chiropractor for a couple of months. But what if we have the same exact broken leg injury, with the only difference being the circumstances of the injured parties themselves? For example, one client might be a blue collar worker whose job requires that he is on his feet all day, lifting heavy items. The other is an office worker who sits at his desk for 90% of the day and can conveniently prop the injured foot up when it begins to ache. The value of the claim for the blue-collar worker who is no longer able to return to his job will be significantly higher than the office worker who can return to work after 8 to 12 weeks of recovery and physical therapy. Determining the value of a client's claim and anticipating what an arbitrator or a jury might do with the claim is thus also very specific to an individual's life circumstances and case.

PITFALLS IN OUR MEDICAL SYSTEM CAN HURT YOUR CLAIM

In addition to valuing a claim, a personal injury attorney must do several very important things as soon as a client has come into the office to retain him. The first important function that we serve is as a phenomenal resource. While it begins with knowing the personal injury process and how it works, it is really also about understanding the pitfalls: how to identify and avoid them when possible and how to correct them should the case encounter one. We need to watch out for the pitfalls because once a mistake is made, it is hard to undo and can have a negative impact on the value of your claim. Many of these pitfalls revolve around the medical care that clients receive, which can be a difficult and complicated issue to navigate these days.

For example, we have many clients who have no health insurance. We believed that with the enactment of the Affordable Care Act, we would begin to see more clients covered by health insurance; the very purpose that prompted the enactment of this law. Unfortunately, we continue to encounter just as many clients today as we did in the past who lack health insurance coverage. When a client does not have health insurance, the problem we face is how to ensure that he receives competent medical care after he has been injured. I believe that a good personal injury attorney must have a network of doctors; a network that includes everything from chiropractors to primary care physicians and specialists, such as orthopedic doctors, neurosurgeons, and pain management doctors. The attorney is then able to have his client seen by one of these doctors under a doctor's lien, even though the client does not have health insurance. In situations like this, the doctor will hold the bill until the case is settled. Some doctors prefer not to wait for their bill to be paid, especially specialists, and in these instances, we can refer clients to networks of doctors who work with a lien-holding company. The lien-holding company will pay the doctors as the bills come in, while waiting to receive their reimbursement until the end of the case. Individuals attempting to handle their own cases typically do not have access to this kind of network themselves.

The danger of postponing medical care because an individual does not have the means to pay medical providers is that an insurance company will always exploit that "treatment gap." A "treatment gap" is the gap in time between when the accident occurred and when a client seeks medical treatment from a doctor. The insurance company will use this gap in treatment to argue that the client was not really injured. The argument is quite simple and goes something like this:

> "Had you been hurt after this accident to the degree that you've claimed, you would certainly have found a way to see a doctor. Attorneys, doctors, and chiropractors advertise on television all day long, so we simply do not buy the argument that you had no idea about where to go for help. You could have made an appointment with your attorney two months earlier and he could have helped you get medical care right away. We believe that you didn't seek medical care because you were simply not hurt at the time, contrary to your claim. At some point, it must have dawned on you that you might be able to get some money

from the accident, which is why you've only now hired an attorney and are claiming to suffer from an injury."

Unfortunately, this really is the insurance company's perspective and they will take any opportunity to use a gap in treatment to argue that you were not truly injured in the accident. Providing insight into proper medical care options available to a client is one very important resource that a good personal injury attorney should provide. Even clients who have health insurance and seek medical care from their primary physician require help at times. Some primary care physicians decline automobile accident cases because they do not wish to become a part of the process. In other words, they do not want to be put in a position that requires them to testify in court about medical care they have provided, only to have someone challenging their every decision about your care. So what can someone do when a primary care physician refuses treatment in these circumstances? This is another instance in which it becomes necessary to rely on your personal injury attorney for guidance. He can provide an invaluable resource: help in obtaining quality medical care, because pitfall number one is medical treatment problems. Gaps in treatment, seeing the wrong physicians, and not obtaining the proper medical tests can be detrimental to your case.

A case I am working on at the moment required that I sit down with my client to discuss a problem he is experiencing with two herniated discs in his neck. His primary care physician referred him to a doctor who could not properly address and treat this injury, a hand specialist, who is trained to consider whether or not he might suffer from carpal tunnel syndrome, which is causing him to experience numbness in his fingers. My client's physician should have referred the client to a spine surgeon, whose expertise allows him to examine the neck injury itself and determine if it is the cause for weakness in my client's hands and other health issues he is having.

Our number one job is to sit down with a client in order to communicate the problems observed with the primary care physician's referral and explain why it is necessary for the injured person to see another specialist for proper diagnosis and treatment of the injuries. If it turns out that this is the reason that the client is suffering, we can then provide assistance in obtaining the proper treatment, which may include surgery, to correct the problem. For whatever reason, the primary care physician in this particular case is pointing my client in the wrong direction, and, even though I do not understand the reasoning behind this decision, my own obligation is to redirect my client in the proper direction using the resources I have built through my years of experience. Though I am not a doctor, I can attest that I have seen thousands of these issues come up in personal injury cases. In this instance, the symptoms that the client is describing matches the symptoms we have seen in many other cases, where the injured party has suffered a herniated disc in the neck.

It is our goal to ensure that this client gets the proper medical treatment he needs so that the insurance company cannot build an argument based on the treatment gap theory. In some cases, the spine surgeon may say that the herniated discs are not creating any additional problems and will refer the client back to his primary care physician, the hand specialist, or another specialist. If that's the case, we have been able to rule out one serious injury and can focus on taking the next step in order to find out what is medically wrong with our client. In the next step, after a client has completed his medical treatment and is as well as can be expected after the injury, the attorney will begin the process of finding a resolution to the case.

It is important that the attorney you have retained to handle your personal injury claim is willing to litigate cases, so that the insurance company is aware that the attorney has a proven track record of doing just that. That alone may be enough to compel the insurance company to pay a fair and just amount, avoiding the need for an attorney to file a lawsuit to make this happen. Nevertheless, if the insurance company refuses to act in a reasonable manner, you can still take confidence in the fact that you have an attorney who is prepared and willing to litigate the claim; one that has the experience and knowledge to navigate you through the entire litigation process and in the end, secure for you the resolution that you need and deserve. These are all crucial things that an attorney brings to the table.

SUBROGATION ISSUES

At the end of the case, an attorney's job is not over. There are still complicated matters regarding settlement that must be addressed and handled prior to the attorney releasing any funds to the client. For example, there may be medical liens and health insurance subrogation issues. Essentially, at the end of your personal injury case, you have a pool of money into which everyone would like to dip their hands. These parties might be hospitals and medical providers with outstanding bills, health insurance companies who want reimbursement for medical bills they paid on your behalf, and any medical liens you may have entered into in order to obtain the medical care you needed for your injuries.

Depending on the type of health insurance policy you hold, your health insurance provider may have a legal right to be reimbursed for any medical bills it paid related to the accident. This right is referred to as a subrogation right. Some health insurance providers do not have any legal right for reimbursement; it just depends on the type of policy, and varies from state to state. For example, if your health insurance policy falls under the ERISA statutes, it has a legal right to be reimbursed for any costs it paid due to an accident covered by a third party. If it does not fall under these statutes, then it depends on state law and the health insurance contract. For instance, Arizona is an anti-subrogation state according to state law, but even though the health insurance provider may not have a subrogation right in Arizona, they will still make the claim. The attorney must sort through this in order to determine who, if anyone, should receive money from the settlement proceeds apart from the attorney and the client. It is our job to both weed out the parties who are not entitled to reimbursement and negotiate all other parties' bills to the lowest amount possible so that the client is left with as much money as possible.

Our client is the one who has been hurt, who has suffered pain due to the accident and whose life has been impacted by his injury; therefore, our client is the one who deserves to be compensated at the end of the day. Sadly, third parties do not care about our client, and see this as merely a business decision to attain as much money as possible in order to make a profit. It is the attorney's responsibility to deal with these issues in the aftermath of the case, because even if the client understands the basic concepts, the process involves a complex set of issues that most clients are unable to deal with on their own.

The at-fault insurance provider just wants to pay the settlement money, cut its losses and move forward. In keeping with this attitude, it will compensate any parties demanding payment, regardless of whether they have a legal right to receive the money. If you have an attorney, third parties will think twice, because of the worry that legal action will be taken against them. I have seen individuals receive the short end of the stick because they have resolved the case on their own and $4,000 that should go to them is paid to the hospital when it should not have been paid to this third party. Once the money has been paid, it is nearly impossible to get it back.

BEWARE OF THESE LANDMINES

There are many landmines that can blow up in a personal injury claim and, unfortunately, those landmines begin as soon as the accident occurs. Because the insurance company is under the assumption that settling a personal injury claim is simply a business transaction, their goal is to resolve the claim as quickly and as inexpensively as possible. To that end, an insurance company does its best to approach individuals with an offer before they have had the opportunity to consult with an attorney.

For example, if an individual is involved in an accident and not seriously injured, he is probably just thankful that he is not bleeding or suffering any broken bones. At this moment, his thoughts are: "Thank goodness I wasn't really hurt. I feel okay. My neck hurts a bit and I have a headache, but I am not in an ambulance in serious condition." He deals with everything that requires his attention at the scene of the accident and then goes home. The insurance adjuster quickly offers a small amount of money, perhaps $1,000, and the individual signs the release to receive the money. It is only days later that he begins to have more pain and sees a doctor. However, by this point, it is too late to pursue a claim as he signed a full and complete release for all claims. Even if you do not believe you are seriously injured, meeting with an attorney and seeing a doctor is always a wise course of action after an accident.

An accident in which neither party appears to be injured presents another landmine. In Tucson, the police will not come to an accident scene if there have been no injuries. When an accident involves serious injury, the police will come to the scene, conduct an investigation and file a report. However, in other cases, they will often advise the parties to exchange information. The landmine in this situation is when individuals do not get complete information about the other driver. If you are involved in an automobile accident and the police do not respond, you need to copy down everything on the other person's driver license and insurance card. If possible, take a picture of both to make sure that you have the information (you can use your cell phone). Write down all of their contact numbers (i.e., cell number, home number, work number, etc.), the vehicle's license tag number and a description of the vehicle.

I had to do this just about a year ago when my wife and I were involved in an accident. Our vehicle was rear-ended by another vehicle, and even though there was no apparent damage to either car, we both felt a pretty hard impact. I have represented clients in these types of accidents where the insurance company tries to argue that it is a low-impact accident, and now I found myself in one and understood that it is possible to experience a hard impact with little to no visible damage to either vehicle.

The young woman driving the other vehicle just wanted to leave, but I said, "Look, here is what we are going to do and if you choose not to do so, that is fine. I've got your name and your license plate number, so if you leave without taking the time to give me all of the information I need, I am going to get a police officer out here, do what I can do to file a report and talk to him about the fact that you were unwilling to stay and exchange information. So let's just do this the easy way. I'd like to see your driver's license and I'm happy to show you mine, even though I don't think this accident was my fault. The reason I want to see your license is to verify that the name on it is the same as the name you've given me, and that the picture on your license is in fact you. I also need to take a picture of it with my cell phone so I can show it to my insurance company. I'll have your address so I'm able to find you, send you a letter, and serve you with a lawsuit if that is what is necessary."

She was not enthusiastic about giving the license to me but eventually she did. Next, I gave her my insurance card and asked to see hers. Again, she was reluctant, but because I had given her mine, she handed me hers. Those are the two main items that you need to see after you've been in an accident. Using your cell phone to take pictures of these documents is an excellent way to preserve the information. It's also important to understand that accidents happen every day and the best way to ensure that you'll be able to work through the process successfully is to be nice to the other party. She did not mean to hit us and there was no reason for me to be confrontational about it. If you are nasty, that is exactly what you get back.

When people are involved in an accident, their adrenaline increases, they are scared and they are not sure if they are injured. In our case, we had our two grandchildren in the car so we were also worried about them. In that scenario, people should take a step back, take a deep breath and think, "Okay, this isn't the end of the world, but what do I need to get before we all drive away and I never see this person again?" Unfortunately, one mistake people often make in these circumstances is to not push the issue when someone says, "My name is Bob and here is my phone number." You need to say, "That alone is unacceptable. I also need to see your driver's license and insurance card and, if you won't let me see them, I will contact the police and pursue whatever course of action I can." I think it might be easier in some places because the police respond to all accidents regardless of whether or not someone is injured. Tucson is perhaps a bit unusual in this regard, but that is, unfortunately, the way it is here. That is why using your cell phone to take pictures of these items at the scene of an accident is a wise move.

It is also crucial that you take pictures of both vehicles to document the damage before they are moved. Once the vehicles leave the scene of the accident, anything can be done to that vehicle and without a police report or photos to document the damage, you are left with nothing more than the conflicting statements from both drivers. Unfortunately, when you begin investigating an accident, the at-fault driver's story often changes, so you have nothing to support your ex-planation as to how the accident happened. We have clients that come in with nothing more than a telephone number because that was all they were given by the other driver. By the time they come to us, they'll have tried several times to contact the individual, who refuses to answer the phone or return messages. Now, if he won't respond to the client, then he will most certainly not respond to our law firm. Without the correct information at our disposal, we do not know whom to serve with a lawsuit, and very few attorneys will spend $600 to

$700 in order to track down a defendant when it has not been ascertained whether he has insurance or assets to pay a claim.

Therefore, the initial landmines in a case of this nature are simply not getting the necessary information or not taking photos of the vehicles at the accident scene. Then you move on to the next landmine: medical treatment issues. This includes seeing the wrong doctors, treatment gaps and self-treatment. People tend to think, "Well, my neck hurts a bit and my back is bothering me a little, but I am okay. I'll just rest, put some ice on it and take some Advil." One week leads to two weeks and then a month has gone by and you've still not seen a doctor, even though the pain has not gone away. When you finally decide to see a doctor, who orders an MRI and discovers that you have a torn rotator cuff, the insurance company uses the treatment gap to argue that the injury was not incurred in the accident and therefore, they are denying coverage. Juries find this to be a persuasive argument, as the insurance companies have learned. This particular landmine, as well as others that can occur throughout the medical treatment process, are well known to attorneys, who also know how to prevent them from becoming a problem in the case. This is why it is important that the client hires an attorney early on in the process, because there is usually nothing we can do after a landmine has blown up and hurt the case.

STATUTE OF LIMITATIONS

Once past the treatment phase, landmines can crop up during the litigation. I do not believe it is possible for someone without an attorney to successfully navigate litigation on his or her own. There are, of course, people who attempt it, but it rarely works out well for them. This final landmine—people handling their own cases—is a huge landmine that often ends badly, with the person receiving nothing for his claim. Take, for example, the statute of limitations issue. Although the insurance company must notify them before the statute of limitations runs, injured victims fail to realize that, as their statute of limitations nears its end, it becomes more and more difficult to find an attorney who will take their case and, if so, they fail to file a lawsuit and they lose their right to recovery.

Another example of how complicated this issue can get involves accidents with government vehicles, whether it be a fire truck, police car, or a truck owned by the city parks department. When a government vehicle is involved, you are now required to give notice of the claim within the deadlines specified for providing notice to government entities and you typically have a much shorter statute of limitations.

In Arizona, notice of the claim must be provided to a government unit within six months from the date of the accident, and in this case, there is a statute of limitations of only one year rather than two years. Again, most individuals assume that because they are dealing with a government entity, they will receive some type of notice warning them before the statute of limitations runs out. What people fail to realize is that attorneys who handle these cases understand these pitfalls and know how to avoid them. However, when a client comes to see us with only a few months before the statute of limitations expires, many times he has already created many problems that we cannot undo.

Through our experience we have discovered that if we take cases that already have these kinds of issues, we end up litigating a case that is not a good one and won't benefit our firm or the client. Therefore, our policy is that if someone comes to us with only three or four months before the statute of limitations expires, we will not take the case, no matter how good it may seem. This is quite simply because we do not have enough time to do what we ethically need to do in order to represent our client.

As attorneys, we must be sure that we don't place the law firm or ourselves in a position where we need to worry about malpractice issues. Insurance companies understand that most law firms have the same perspective. If a case does not settle early for a small amount, the insurance company moves on to its next tactic, which is to allow the case to drag on for as long as possible knowing that most people who are not represented by an attorney will make mistakes that will ultimately benefit the company. People who represent themselves will inevitably get caught in these types of pitfalls and landmines.

The insurance company hopes that the case will get pushed out until the statute of limitations is about to expire and the insurance company can count on the fact that you will not be able to hire an attorney in time to reverse the damage. Now the insurance company can get out cheaply because, rather than returning phone calls or addressing the claim, they will choose to wait until the statute of limitations is about to run out before they offer a small amount of money to settle the claim. They know that if you do not take that little bit of money, you are pretty much out of luck. This is a grim reality that someone who has been hurt in an accident and has a legitimate claim must face. People who fail to retain an attorney early in the case are basically in a position of being forced to settle the claim on their own before the statute of limitations expires, because the likelihood of finding an attorney at this late stage in the process is very low.

THE INSURANCE COMPANY WILL ONLY PAY IF THERE IS SOMEONE WHO IS ABLE TO MAKE THEM PAY

During the past 11 years, there have been two cases that have stuck with me, because they have shown me that the insurance side of personal injury claims is nothing more than just a business. These companies are not concerned with taking care of people who have been injured or with fairly compensating people for their damages. I think this is one of the most compelling reasons as to why people need a personal injury attorney: the insurance company will only pay if there is someone who is able or willing to make them pay. An experienced attorney can help you to avoid the common pitfalls and landmines that frequently crop up in a case and will take on the insurance company in an adversarial manner in order to get you the compensation you deserve.

We represented a young man who attended college here in Tucson. He and his friend were both 21 years old and had been partying and bar-hopping during the course of the evening. At about one o'clock in the morning, as they were traveling down a road on the outskirts of Tucson, the driver lost control of the vehicle. Our client was ejected from the vehicle as it rolled over. The driver managed to get out of the vehicle, didn't see his friend and began walking down the road. Even though he knew his friend was injured, he realized that he would be in trouble for driving while intoxicated, so he simply walked away from the accident. About a mile down the road, someone stopped to see if he needed help. The person offered to drive him to the hospital or call the police but the driver was insistent that he take him home. The individual repeatedly asked him if he could take him to the hospital or get help because it was apparent that the driver was in bad shape, but the driver continued to decline the offer. During this exchange, he never mentioned that his friend had been in the car with him.

The person who found the driver noticed a sheriff's car, which turned out to be an off-duty sheriff's deputy going home after a shift, and flagged it down. When the deputy spoke to the driver, the driver told the deputy that his friend, our client, was driving when they had an accident, but refused to tell him where the accident had happened, where his friend was, or where the car had been left. They actually had to call out a helicopter to examine heat signatures in order to determine where the accident had occurred. Our client was finally located and transported to the hospital, where it was discovered that he had been paralyzed from the waist down. The driver continued to maintain that he had not been driving at the time of the accident and so he was never charged with a DUI. The county attorney's office never pursued criminal charges against the driver because he stuck with his story, and his insurance company decided to fight us to the bitter end. Ultimately, we litigated and made them pay. However, it was a long and costly process for our client.

We had to hire an accident reconstruction expert and a biomechanics engineer to prove that our client had not been driving that night when the accident occurred. Most of the time in serious accident cases like this one, there is not sufficient insurance money to cover all of the plaintiff's damages. Rather than simply doing the right thing and compensating our client, the insurance company saw an opportunity to fight us, due to the other person's statement, and were more than happy to spend that money to fight the claim. I do not think most people understand that insurance companies are not there to step in and try to help you piece everything back together after a horrible accident. This case is a vivid illustration and reminder that insurance companies are just a business and that is how these cases work.

The second case that makes this point, and has stuck with me over the years, involved a young family. Our client was driving through a four-way stop with his wife and nine-month old baby when a drunk driver, who had run the stop sign at 50 miles per hour, struck the car. The driver, who had just left a university basketball game, did not stop after the collision and was actually chased down by several vehicles in the vicinity. When the driver finally pulled over in a parking lot, one of his pursuers held him on the ground until the police arrived. Though the parents were not seriously injured in the accident, their baby suffered a head injury that required her to stay in the ICU for several weeks and undergo surgery. From that moment, she suffered cognitive and behavioural issues due to the trauma, and at four years of age, she was still unable to speak. It was a very sad situation.

The drunk driver happened to have a very large commercial insurance policy on his vehicle. His insurance company argued that it takes some children longer than others to speak, and that certain children are prone to bad behavior and she was simply acting out. The stance they took was to refuse to pay this family any money until they sued the insurance company. The insurance company forced the law firm to do everything required in order to work this case up and prepare it for trial, just to give the case the value that it deserved to have, based on the facts. It was as if the insurance company was saying, "Doug Zanes, we will give you every opportunity to make a mistake in the process of preparing this case for trial and we will only pay this family what they deserve if you avoid making these mistakes." So that is exactly what we did.

Over a two-year period, they made us dot our I's and cross our T's and do everything necessary and do it all well by spending about $100,000 hiring experts and preparing the case before they were willing to pay any amount. From my perspective, it is quite honestly an ugly, nasty business because when someone has been significantly injured by a drunk driver, the insurance company should step in, take care of you and pay a fair settlement. Unfortunately, that is just not how it works.

THE INSURANCE COMPANY IS NOT YOUR FRIEND, NOR IS IT YOUR ENEMY; IT'S SIMPLY A BUSINESS LOOKING TO MAKE A PROFIT

I would like everyone to understand that we must deal with insurance companies whenever we are injured, whether it is riding a bicycle, crossing a road or driving on the interstate, and the insurance company has just one goal in mind: to use any argument they can make to lower the value of the claim. Whether it is accusing the victim of being partially negligent in causing the accident or blaming the victim for not taking action to avoid it entirely, the insurance company will drag out the process as long as possible in the hope that you will inadvertently make a mistake and lower the value of your claim. The insurance company is not your friend and it is not your enemy; it is simply a business looking to make a profit. Unless a person truly understands this concept and the business end of the claims process, he or she really needs someone who has the knowledge to help him or her.

A good attorney is committed to looking out for your best interests, and to that end, he will do whatever is necessary, even reducing the contingency fee, to get the resolution that you deserve. I know many personal injury attorneys who are not only good trial attorneys, they are good people. That is the kind of person you should seek out when searching for a personal injury attorney, because he or she, unlike the insurance company, will work hard with your best interests in mind. Our law firm operates from the perspective that when a client hires us, he has placed himself in our care and will benefit from our guidance and protection. This is how we always approach cases and our clients. I believe in my heart that this is truly what anyone who has been injured needs. If an attorney with these qualities represents you, you will win in the end.

(This content should be used for informational purposes only. It does not create an attorney-client relationship with any reader and should not be construed as legal advice. If you need legal advice, please contact an attorney in your community who can assess the specifics of your situation.)

3

VALUABLE INSIGHTS INTO MEDICAL MALPRACTICE

by Howard D. Mishkind, Esq.

Howard D. Mishkind, Esq.
Mishkind Law Firm Co., L.P.A.
Cleveland, Ohio

Howard is President and Founder of the Mishkind Law Firm Co., L.P.A. His practice is concentrated primarily in the area of personal injury litigation, consisting of the representation of injured patients and their families in medical malpractice, legal malpractice, and catastrophic injuries arising out of motor vehicle collisions.

He has been managing medical malpractice and personal injury claims for decades. He never forgets, however, that each of his clients is facing these issues for the first time. He understands how difficult it is to cope with the personal and financial losses caused by negligence. He takes the time to listen to his client's concerns, explain his or her legal options, and get any questions answered.

With Howard, it's personal. His clients are not just cases to him but people who have been harmed through no fault of their own. He has been representing the people in Ohio for over 30 years.

VALUABLE INSIGHTS INTO MEDICAL MALPRACTICE

When doctors and patients hear the term "Medical Malpractice," it is often misunderstood and feared for reasons that will be discussed during this chapter. So much has been written about medical malpractice. In some ways, a claim for medical malpractice is similar to other types of injury claims. In other respects, it is substantially different. Medical negligence claims have special rules and requirements that are unlike other personal injury cases.

When a patient receives medical treatment in a hospital, doctor's office, nursing home, or rehabilitation facility, complications can arise which, in turn, can result in injury. Patient safety should always be the No. 1 goal of any medical treatment. Good communication between the medical staff and the patient is of critical importance - whether the patient is undergoing a simple blood test, an x-ray, a diagnostic test (such as an EKG or a mammogram), or surgical care. Every patient should be equipped with as much information as possible before making an informed decision about a recommended course of treatment so that he or she knows whether the treatment is worth the risk that many medical procedures carry. In a perfect world, where time was not a limiting factor, the patient and the doctor would have sufficient time to review the patient's history, as well as any current complaints and limitations that the condition seems to be causing, so that they can carefully devise a well-planned course of treatment.

Obviously, the best way to avoid being injured by medical care is to know as much about your doctor, the hospital where he or she will be treating you, and the various tests and procedures that will be performed. Often, patients are reluctant to ask questions in advance or to speak up and ask why something is being done or administered. The days of total and complete trust in your doctor to the point that you, as the patient, blindly agree to everything that he recommends should be a thing of the past. Patients need to be actively involved in their healthcare and not assume that the doctor knows all of their symptoms or that his initial diagnosis is accurate.

You truly need to speak up and stay alive. Avoiding preventable medical errors is a joint undertaking between the patient and the doctor. The more you know and the more you act as an informed medical consumer, the better off you will be. But don't think for a moment that you are not entitled to second opinions or to question why something is being recommended. Don't worry about asking why something went wrong during surgery and do expect that you are entitled to honest answers. The patient should have as much information as possible before the treatment or surgery in order to determine if the injury that occurs as a result of the treatment was the result of a medical error during the procedure or a known and recognized potential risk or complication that could not have been prevented.

HOW CAN I BEST BE PREPARED?

If a patient understands the goal or intended outcome of the medical procedure, from the risks of procedural complications to the benefits of having the procedure, he or she is in a better position to decide whether or not to consult with a medical malpractice attorney. As the saying goes, "an educated consumer is the best customer." An educated patient is usually in a better position to stay safe and avoid being harmed by preventable medical errors. An informed patient can better recognize when a medical error has occurred, why the injury occurred, whether or not the injury will be long-standing, or if it is a temporary injury without a major future impact. After experiencing an injury, the patient may believe that there is a need to consult with a medical malpractice attorney if the doctor or medical provider is not providing sufficient answers about the occurrence of the injury or complication. In that instance, the patient should find an attorney who specializes in cases involving the type of injury in question, whether it is an infection, amputation, stroke, or a failed repair of a broken bone, etc.

Let me be clear: not all injuries that occur in a medical setting are the result of medical negligence. In most states, including Ohio (where I practice), it takes more than a bad result for a medical procedure to qualify as a valid medical malpractice claim. A number of elements must be proven before determining whether the injury was due to medical negligence. Medical negligence does not mean that the doctor or nurse or other healthcare provider intended to cause harm. Malpractice means negligence. It means that a mistake was made that, if the doctor or healthcare provider had been exercising reasonable care, most likely would have been avoided. It does not mean the doctor intended to cause harm, that he is incompetent, or that he will lose his license. It means that his medical mistake caused a patient injury that otherwise probably would not have occurred. The law does not require proof beyond a reasonable doubt or to a certainty.

The law in tort claims requires proof by preponderance of evidence, which means more likely than not. Medical malpractice claims and other personal injury claims are torts, meaning a civil wrongful act resulting in injury. It is not a crime, even though the term "malpractice" sounds like it means the doctor must be found guilty of negligence. This is not so. The law requires that the doctor must be shown to have been negligent when comparing his care to that which other doctors in similar circumstances would have done. It does not mean the doctor committed a crime, but so many people feel that it is unfair to file a medical malpractice claim when they are injured due to their basic lack of understanding as to the elements of such a claim. If someone causes harm and that harm is both serious and due to negligence, our system of justice provides for a remedy to attempt to make the injured party whole. The same applies when that negligence is caused by a healthcare provider.

WHAT IS MEDICAL MALPRACTICE?

If a patient is injured during medical care and the injury is likely to cause substantial or additional physical deformity, emotional distress, and/or a permanent disability, he or she should consult with a medical malpractice attorney to determine if the injury was preventable and whether or not there is merit to investigate a possible medical negligence claim. Many times, the attorney will conclude that the client does not have a valid medical claim or that proving the injury claimed to have been caused by the medical care given would not have occurred anyway. The process of investigating a medical claim starts with an understanding of the medicine and if the injury that occurred can be proven to be due to a violation of the "standard of care." ("Standard of care" is the magical phrase used in medical malpractice cases to prove negligence.) One has to prove that the doctor had a duty to act or take action on behalf of the patient and then it must be shown either that the conduct on the part of the doctor was within the standard of care or fell below the standard of care. Often, this element of proof becomes the focus of the battle of experts as to what was the standard of care (the duty of the doctor) and whether what he did or did not do violated that standard.

In this day and age, we all expect to receive world class care or the best of care. But we are frequently disappointed by what happens and more often to learn that what the doctor did might not have been the best of care or even the type of care that the expert would have provided, but it was still within the standard of care. Frequently, the care that the doctor provided was less than optimal and might even earn him or her a "C" grade if he were being judged. There are experts who will testify that the care which resulted in the injury met a minimum standard of care and that they can't find that the doctor fell below that "C" grade. I know what you are thinking at this point, but while we hear about getting the greatest of care through advertising and rating systems and what we ultimately receive when we are under the doctor's care often falls far short of that "A" grade, it still may not be considered to be negligent or a violation of the standard of care.

Many people erroneously assume that when medical negligence occurs, the attorney must prove that the doctor *intended* to cause the bad result or acted with reckless disregard for the patient's safety. Medical negligence is nothing more than negligence in the setting of medical care. If it can be proven that the medical provider (i.e., doctor, nurse, physical therapist, other healthcare providers, etc.) failed to do what a reasonable and prudent medical provider would have done under like or similar circumstances, the patient is one step closer toward establishing a medical malpractice claim.

The second step is to prove that the negligence was the legal cause or "proximate cause" of the injury. A medical provider can fail to order the proper diagnostic test or prescribe the wrong medicine to a patient. However, it still must be proven that, more likely than not, the injury would not have occurred if the proper test had been ordered or if the patient had received the correct medication. In Ohio, as in most states, this does not need to be proven with absolute certainty. It's only necessary to prove to a slightly higher degree than a 50% medical probability that, with the correct medication or correct test, the injury could have been avoided. It is not necessary to prove with certainty that the injury would have been avoided. If it cannot be proven that the injury or complication occurred because the test was not ordered in a timely manner, or because the patient received the wrong medication, there is no basis for a medical malpractice claim.

Whenever a patient sustains an injury due to received medical care, he should not automatically assume that the bad outcome was caused by medical malpractice. However, he should not be afraid to ask questions and to consult with a medical malpractice attorney to explore his options and to determine if he has a basis for a medical malpractice claim. When I first meet with a potential client, I want to gather as much information as possible: namely, the reason for the patient's treatment by a doctor, the reason for the patient's stay in the hospital, the number of doctors who have seen the patient, and the patient's medical history. After this, I need to identify the injury that the patient believes was caused by the medical provider's negligence. I have found that what a patient believes to be the injury caused by the negligent care and what I believe I can prove to a jury to be the injury are often distinctly different. It therefore requires a careful discussion with the client so that he or she understands the realities of trying to prove an injury that a jury will understand and be willing to compensate you for. Hurt feelings or other improper conduct on the part of a doctor or nurse often causes patients to consult with an attorney, but it is not that conduct by itself that will result in legal action. There may be other options for the patient to pursue with local or state agencies if the conduct is unprofessional, but it may not rise to the level of a medical negligence claim.

I like to simplify this step as much as possible. The simpler the client's perception is concerning the cause of the injury, the better I can ascertain the potential basis for a malpractice case. As attorneys trained in medical legal jargon and medical legal evidence, it is easy for us to zero in on what the client is truly saying when he or she is given the opportunity to explain what happened in plain terms.

In many cases, clients have what we refer to as "comorbidity"— namely, a long list of pre-existing medical conditions that may complicate the patient's recovery, such as diabetes, peripheral vascular disease, and hypertension. Therefore, if a patient suffers an injury, attorneys must determine if that injury was due to the patient's underlying medical condition. The simplest way to ascertain this is to ask the following question: "Would a healthy person have had the same result, or did the patient's other medical condition(s) have an impact on the outcome?"

In some cases, the injury could be the result of the medical provider's failure to take the patient's medical history into account and to take extra precautions to avoid a bad outcome. For example, patients who develop cancer are often hesitant to reach out to a medical malpractice attorney if they are smokers. While smoking can increase the risk of some cancers, the issue does not solely center on the existence and length of the smoking habit: rather, the issue revolves around the development and timing of symptoms associated with the cancer, such as hemoptysis, in which the patient starts coughing up blood. Important information includes the timing of doctor visits and whether or not the doctor ordered x-rays or other tests. If the x-ray was misread or the doctor failed to order diagnostic tests, the doctor cannot blame the patient or say that the patient's habit of smoking was the cause of the cancer. The central issue doesn't hinge on the patient's contribution to the disease; rather, it hinges on whether or not the doctor failed to correctly diagnose the disease as early as possible and whether, with earlier diagnosis and treatment, the patient would likely have had a better outcome. In other words, was the patient in the right place to have his cancer diagnosed and treated so that he likely would have been cured or given a better chance of survival?

Timing is especially important in cancer cases, since a late diagnosis can lead to the cancer metastasizing or spreading to other organs. That is, after all, why patients trust doctors to diagnose a disease early on: so that the patient can receive the right treatment for the disease. If a doctor fails to diagnose a medical condition, or renders a misdiagnosis which is later reversed by a correct diagnosis (made months or years later), a medical malpractice attorney can help determine if the outcome would have been the same if the doctor had made the correct diagnosis at the beginning of the patient's visits to the doctor's office.

Due to the ever increasing types of medical errors that occur (both preventable and otherwise) and are reported by medical journals, it seems that doctors are fearful of their patients when a bad outcome occurs. How often have you heard someone say, "After my surgery, my doctor never came in to see me or to explain why things didn't go right?" It is at this point that it appears that communication between the patient and the physician often breaks down and distrust occurs. Doctors often view every patient as a potential lawsuit; when something goes wrong, doctors are reluctant to discuss the situation. Many times, risk managers at hospitals tell their doctors and nurses not to admit fault or assume responsibility or to even apologize when something goes wrong.

The fear that a simple apology will result in a patient running to a lawyer is unfounded and often is all that a patient needs to hear. Giving and receiving information is a very delicate process when someone has suffered an unanticipated injury. While it may be understandable due to human nature, a patient should refrain from yelling at or getting into an argument with the doctor. Accusations by the patient will only cause the doctor to become defensive and refuse to admit or apologize for the mistake. In most cases, the doctor will tell the patient that the procedure was conducted exactly as it should have been, and that the injury sustained was a common occurrence in this type of procedure (even if it only occurs in 1–2% of all cases). Either the doctor has no explanation for the outcome or does not know why the surgery was not successful. Furthermore, most average patients have no way of determining by the doctor's mannerism whether or not the doctor is being entirely candid and forthright in these explanations.

The first thing that a patient needs to do is determine the context of the injury through certain questions. Will this injury heal in a few days, weeks, or months? Is it likely that there will be permanent residual complications affecting the patient's ability to perform normal daily activities or to take care of him/herself? Will the injury affect the patient's ability to return to work or to enjoy pre-injury activities? How will this injury affect the patient's future as a whole? An informed patient is in a better position to listen as objectively as possible to the doctor, regarding the reason for the injury and the prognosis for the future. Doctors cannot guarantee that the outcome will be perfect, but patients should still strive to approach the matter intelligently if the outcome does not meet the patient's expectations. Just as you want your doctor to listen to you and understand your medical issue, you also have every right and expectation that your doctor will explain how recovery from a procedure should proceed and whether he has any concerns that the outcome might not be as predicted.

Don't be afraid to ask questions and, if necessary, consult with an attorney as early as possible so that you know the types of questions you should ask. Most attorneys who handle these types of claims want to help as early as possible. Frequently, that help is to provide guidance so that the doctor–patient relationship can be saved and restored so that you know what kinds of answers are likely truthful and what kind of answers are evasive. When you are told it could take a year before we know whether you will heal, you should be mindful that such an answer may be an attempt to have you sit back and let your legal rights expire.

Attorneys always want to be very sensitive to the fact that this is a personal injury: a physical injury to the patient or, in the case of wrongful death, the loss of a client's loved one. It is also important that you do not hide information from your attorney when asked about your medical history because past medical history can be and often is extremely important in evaluating the nature of your claim. As attorneys, we do not want to put anyone through the ordeal of a lawsuit when a loved one has died unless we truly believe we can make a difference for the family and protect others in the future from a similar occurrence taking place. If the likelihood of winning at trial is limited and the costs of pursing a claim make the process unworkable, your attorney should explain what to expect so that you do not add insult to misery by going through a trial only to have the doctor or hospital be found not to be negligent.

Incidentally, I frequently speak to clients soon after an injury has occurred and tell them that no malpractice case can possibly give them back what they have lost if, in fact, there was malpractice. That is why it is so important for patients to be informed and to discuss the matter with their doctors. The patient should ask pointed questions to gather as much information as possible about the injury and the prognosis for the future, consider the doctor's answers, and decide if those answers make sense. If the answers seem "funny" or the doctor is being evasive, I encourage people to get a second opinion rather than immediately pursuing a lawsuit for medical malpractice.

An experienced medical malpractice attorney can guide the patient through the process of asking questions and receiving information from the patient's physician in order to determine the potential for a medical malpractice claim. Based on experience, if an ethical and experienced attorney sees that the bad outcome is not likely going to develop into a medical malpractice claim, he will help his client see why. He will help explain why the outcome in this type of case is not likely to result in compensation. As patient advocates, fighting to protect the rights of those injured by medical mistakes that kill and seriously harm hundreds of thousands of patients each year, we can't change the outcome but can only try to prevent it from occurring in the future and making sure that the damages and future costs are assigned to the responsible party so that Medicaid and other public assistance is not called in to pay for the costs that should be borne by the responsible party. When doctors and hospitals are excused from paying for harm caused, we all suffer and we all pay more for medical care. When doctors and hospitals are made to pay what they should, patients are saved the costs of increased medical care.

We realize that we can't turn the hands of the clock back on the injury or death and that our system of justice does not operate by an eye for an eye. Our system of justice can only compensate for the harm and losses caused and attempt to hold the responsible party accountable for the damages. A doctor or a hospital should not be treated any differently in the eyes of the law than you or I would if we caused injury by driving negligently or when we are negligent in maintaining our property and injury occurs. But the reality is that, because of the evidence that has to be established through expert medical testimony, proving these types of cases is extremely expensive and many patients don't even know that they have a claim.

We hear from neighbors, friends, relatives, or other sources so many "medical malpractice myths" that many people start out favoring doctors in these cases. Once the myths of medical malpractice cases are understood and the public realizes that there is too much medical malpractice and not too many medical malpractice lawsuits, patients will be treated fairly and the political rhetoric of why malpractice cases are bad will be defeated. As a patient safety advocate, the hardest part of my job is educating honest hard working Ohioans the horror, the unfairness and the pain of how tort reform can be. To the family of a patient abused in a nursing home, I have had to explain how the nursing home would not settle their case of obvious negligence for an amount that the family considered fair because the nursing home realized that the maximum it would have to pay (due to limits imposed on pain and suffering) if it loses is $250,000.00.

Several myths about medical negligence and malpractice suits continue to spread like wild fire. They are popular falsehoods that cause an unfair shift of responsibility from the healthcare field to the injured patients. Why? Because big business interests have been successful in convincing everyone that rising insurance costs are due to too many lawsuits. Not true!!

The lies and myths spread by those that believe tort reform is needed and is good for society push their agenda to limit the ability of injured patients to seek compensation for medical malpractice in Ohio and throughout the nation. Many of you reading this are probably secretly in favor of limiting compensation to injured Americans caused by medical negligence. What if, you or a loved one was injured and you couldn't recover compensation for your injuries or you were told that your baby's lifetime of pain and suffering was limited to

$500,000.00? What if you were injured and were told you could only recover $250,000.00 for your loss of normal enjoyment of life and your pain and suffering because your injury was not a permanent and substantial injury? What if…?

A number of citizens believe that when doctors enter the courtroom, they find themselves at a clear disadvantage. This myth holds that doctors are entering the courtroom to predetermined scowls and leaving broken, maligned professionals. However, this is anything but the truth. It is extremely difficult in Ohio to get a doctor to testify against a doctor even when the negligence is clear and beyond debate. While patients and their families suffer due to avoidable injuries, doctors feel like they are being taken advantage of. Not true!

Study after study by medical professionals and published in peer reviewed journals such as the *Archives of Internal Medicine* and *CHEST*, to name a few, have found that contrary to popular belief many hold, doctors are not the victims of a medical malpractice bias as their defense attorneys like to claim. In fact, a study entitled "Outcomes of Medical Malpractice Litigation against US Physicians," has found that in cases which go to verdict, almost 80% were judged in favor of the physician.

Finally, the widespread belief propagated by tort reform advocates which states that these lawsuits are growing out of control and increasingly burdening the court system has also been proven false. In fact, medical malpractice filings are drastically down, in large part because the current laws have made many otherwise meritorious claims cost prohibitive. The compensation caps have driven thousands of injured patients away from being able to hold a doctor or hospital responsible because the costs to get to court and to a jury verdict outweigh the potential recovery in many cases so the doctor or hospital get away without any consequences. The number of lawsuits filed is generally trending down in many states, thus refuting this baseless myth.

The American Association for Justice, reports that despite hundreds of thousands of medical injuries that take place each year, only about one in eight of these patients actually files a claim. Even though claim numbers are dropping and jury verdict payouts and settlements have also declined, victims of medical malpractice are continually finding increased difficulty when it comes to receiving fair compensation for their injuries.

Now that I hopefully have your attention, let's get back to what you should do in the event that you are courageous enough to realize that something might have gone wrong and that the truth might be hard to come by. I advise my clients to buy a notebook and write down as much as they can when they are in the hospital or encounter a concerning issue so that things are kept in an orderly manner, and everything that has occurred throughout the procedure can be better understood if and when it is appropriate to review with an attorney. They should mark down what they are told by the doctor (or other healthcare providers) regarding treatment, testing, and prognosis. After all, the hospital and the doctor create records that should accurately reflect what happened and, as a patient, you should be in the best position—especially if you have family or friends with you—to be able to confirm or refute what was said or when the doctor or nurse came in to treat, explain, or respond to your issues. If possible, I advise my clients to have someone with them at every doctor's appointment. Even the most organized person can forget key details that are essential to the case. Furthermore, it is advisable to have a witness who can listen to the conversations between the patient and the doctor, and attest to the notes in the patient's log.

Clients should continue to keep this log of events all the way through the trial. After months or years, memories begin to fade. The doctor will have medical records to refer to in court. Therefore, clients should have their own written record to help them remember key points that happened throughout course of the medical procedure and the malpractice action. Contemporaneous notes that a patient makes can perhaps disprove statements made by the doctor, or substantiate information that the patient conveyed to the doctor. For example, "The doctor did not write down in my records that I reported blood in my urine, but I reported this symptom to the doctor on May 7th and again on June 1st."

I am not insinuating that a doctor would purposefully misrepresent the records. However, due to the fast-paced setting of many doctors' offices and the fact that many hospital residents are overworked and under the gun, there are times when what is said in a patient's room or in the examining room may not be properly noted in the patient's records. Therefore, I encourage all patients to prepare a timeline in great detail: what was said, when it was said, the nature of the patient's complaints, and what the doctor did in response to those complaints. I do not advocate sitting in front of the doctor and writing down every word. However, once patients leave the office, they should take a moment to jot down the details, adding these notes to their timeline when they get home. By doing this, patients are not specifically looking for a medical malpractice claim, they are simply being responsible patients and preparing for the future, in case something goes wrong. If they must file a claim later, it's helpful to have contemporaneous notes of the doctor's words and actions pre- and post-surgery, as well as the potential complications and necessary instructions which the patient received and reviewed with the medical staff.

Patients should not include personal opinions in the log; entries must be strictly factual. For example, a patient should write, "Dr. Smith advised me to avoid eating anything after midnight," rather than, "Grumpy old Dr. Smith will not let me have anything to eat after midnight." Patients must keep in mind that they are composing their own medical records, in case there is something important missing from their official medical records at the doctor's office or hospital. This will help them to counter incorrect evidence in their medical records, while in court. Frequently, attorneys are placed in a "he said/she said" situation with only memories to guide their legal decisions, and unfortunately, memories are not like fine wines: they do not get better over time.

Let me assure you: most competent medical malpractice attorneys can very easily determine whether or not someone is trying to create a baseless claim. On the other hand, preparing to deal with a potential complication by knowing the questions to ask and taking proper notes can help patients remember exactly what was explained. This includes anything that was left out that should have been explained prior to the treatment, procedure, or surgery. Even though this timeline will be discoverable by the other party if a lawsuit is filed, a log is very helpful even during treatment. It allows the patient to question the doctor's orders to do "A" one day and then to do something different ("B") the next day.

In short, a patient's log or timeline should be honest and factual for two reasons. The first reason deals with the patient's safety and health. In the unlikely event that something does go wrong in the procedure, an accurate timeline means that the patient is not dealing from a purely subjective, emotional standpoint. Rather, there is a factual basis for the patient's questions. The second reason for a factual timeline is that this timeline will be discoverable in a lawsuit. The opposing side is entitled to a copy of the patient's notes, and it is better to have simple facts to share rather than emotions. However, in the event that the patient's attorney asked the patient to produce a diary strictly for the attorney to use as work product, the timeline is considered privileged information that the opposing side cannot subpoena. There is often a fine line between what is privileged and what is discoverable, but this topic is far beyond the scope of this chapter.

No one knows your health better than you do or knows how things have changed due to your medical condition. Be smart and be prepared. The more information you have, the better you will be able to determine if your current situation should be discussed with a lawyer. If you have questions or you are unsure, contact a medical malpractice attorney and ask him if he will review your timeline or journal. Being offered a written history makes the communication to the attorney much more efficient, enjoyable, and pleasant for the potential client.

TYPES OF CLAIMS

Just as there are many types of personal injury claims, there are many types of medical malpractice claims. Failure to diagnose is a frequent cause of medical malpractice claims. Failing to diagnose a medical condition in its early stages can result in a worsening condition. For example, failing to diagnose cancer in its early stages allows the cancer to progress, making the prognosis much worse. Likewise, failing to diagnose coronary artery disease in the early stages, when treatment may be more effective, can mean the difference between minimal treatment with medicine or less invasive procedures such as coronary stenting and a major coronary artery bypass surgery, myocardial infarction, or death.

Misdiagnosis is another common form of medical negligence and is frequently due to a similarity in symptoms between differing diseases. A patient may be misdiagnosed in the emergency room with GERD (gastro esophageal reflux disease). This patient is promptly sent home without any tests being performed. Rather than suffering from GERD, the patient actually has a massive coronary or myocardial infarction (a condition in which the heart muscle dies). Because of the misdiagnosis, the patient is treated for the wrong condition. As a result, a bad and avoidable outcome may occur.

Differential diagnosis is common in medical care. Identifying the possible causes of a patient's symptoms and identifying those causes that can be life-threatening and ruling out the life-threatening causes before concluding that the non-life-threatening condition is the answer, is always best. The patient could die before receiving help or may face a much worse prognosis than if the condition were diagnosed properly in the first place.

Surgical errors are a third and common type of medical malpractice. Consider a patient whose "hollow viscous" is perforated during abdominal surgery. This area contains the vital organs such as the colon, spleen, and kidneys. If one of the vital organs or a major artery is nicked during surgery, the patient could develop an infection due to the laceration. Of course, this is one of the risks of abdominal surgery. The question is "Was that error preventable?" The answer to this question will determine the continuation of the patient's claim. Delay in performing surgery can also lead to a malpractice claim. If the patient has symptoms that require surgery and the surgery is delayed, the patient can experience life-threatening complications due to the delay.

We see these types of cases when a patient presents to a hospital on a weekend, during shift changes, or when residents (doctors-in-training) are just coming on to a new rotation and the patient is not given the kind of urgent or emergent care he needs that would have occurred if he were treated during the week when the full staff of doctors was available.

The fourth major malpractice claim occurs when the medical staff or the doctors fail to respond in a timely manner to a surgical error. A surgery patient may begin to show signs of infection such as a sudden change in his blood count, an increased heart rate, high fever, abdominal distention or hardness in the abdomen. These are all signs of possible sepsis—a dangerous infection of the blood—which can migrate to the vital organs and become fatal if not treated quickly. Doctors and medical staff are aware of the symptoms of sepsis and know that treatment must begin at the first sign of the bacteria. If left untreated, the infection will move to the lungs or the kidneys, and the doctor jeopardizes his ability to prevent permanent damage and save the patient.

Prescription errors are a fifth and common type of medical malpractice case, even though many of these situations go unnoticed or unreported by patients. One common error is a negative interaction between a current medication and a newly prescribed medication. Attorneys also see prescription errors in hospitals, when a doctor has prescribed a medication but transcribed it incorrectly. The nurse then misreads the directions and gives the patient the wrong dosage or even the wrong medicine. These mistakes may result in various complications to the patient's health and recovery.

The sixth type of error is found when patients suffer injuries because of basic communication issues between the nurse and the doctor, between two doctors, or between shift changes. If a doctor happens to be in the emergency room toward the end of a shift and another emergency room doctor is taking over, it is critical to have a clear report from the attending physician to the new physician. It is equally necessary to note records in the patient's medical chart about anything that has happened during the past 8- or 12-hour shift, especially when there is a weekend shift change coming up. Due to the use of electronic records, attorneys often see system errors occur when there are many different healthcare providers involved in a patient's care. Frankly, it is amazing that there are not *more* breakdowns in communication, when so many people are working with the same patient. Full medical records and proper communication are essential elements in avoiding preventable medical errors.

A seventh type of medical malpractice occurs in the failure to perform appropriate testing. Consider a doctor who is presented with a patient at risk for stroke due to heart valve issues or a blockage in one of the carotid arteries (arteries that lead from the neck to the brain). In many of those cases, the doctor fails to do the appropriate tests after a patient displays what is called "Jugular Venous Distention," a condition in which the vein in the neck is visibly throbbing. Failing to recommend a course of action, such as a stent or a carotid endarterectomy (to remove plaque from the artery before it breaks off and causes a stroke), is a common medical error. A medical condition entitled Transient Ischemic Attacks (TIA) can also lead to medical malpractice. In these cases, the patients' symptoms are usually evident to their primary physicians. However, the physician fails to order tests to determine the extent of the carotid disease, so the patient suffers a stroke that could have been prevented if the doctor ordered the necessary medical tests. With patients who have atrial fibrillation, the atrium in the upper chambers of the heart can develop blood clots that can lead to stroke. Those patients must be on a blood thinner to prevent stroke. However, blood thinners (such as Coumadin and Warfarin) have associated risks that require the doctor to monitor the patient, to make sure that complications do not arise from the patient taking the medication.

Anesthesia malpractice is the eighth type of medical malpractice. Pre-anesthesia examination is one of the numerous opportunities for medical errors. If a person with a prior surgery is scheduled to undergo general anesthesia—meaning that an endotracheal tube will be inserted down his throat—he will essentially be asleep during the procedure. Even in cases where the patient receives "twilight" anesthesia so that he is not fully asleep during the procedure, it is essential that the patient's medical history be reviewed and examined prior to ad- ministering the anesthesia, so that the anesthesiologist ad- ministers the proper medication. Furthermore, a careful exam- ination of the patient's neck and upper airway must be conducted to determine the difficulty of intubating or extubating the patient's airway after surgery. In the cases of patients who have had chronic obstructive pulmonary disease, it is frequently difficult to extubate the airway, and these patients may ex- perience difficulty breathing on their own after surgery.

An anesthesiologist has the duty to keep the patient alive during surgery, as the medical professional in control of the patient's airway and breathing. An anesthesiologist chooses which anesthetic agent to give the patient to put him to sleep, monitors the patient's vital signs during the surgery, makes adjustments as necessary to the anesthesia, and reverses the process once the surgery is completed. Since there is so much room for error, the pre-examination with the anesthesiologist or the certified registered nurse anesthetist (CRNA) prior to surgery is vital, to ensure that the anesthesiologist can obtain all of the medical information necessary to protect the patient before, during, and after surgery. The anesthesiologist must be prepared for potential problems by having the proper equipment and medications in the operating room.

These are several other types of medical malpractice cases that our firm handles related to anesthesia:

- Laryngospasms: In this condition, the patient's airway closes, and the patient becomes hypoxic or anoxic due to inadequate oxygen flow. The anesthesiologist must quickly give the patient an injection to carefully relax the larynx so that the patient does not go into respiratory arrest.

- Sleep apnea or other respiratory problems: After surgery, a patient is transferred to the PACU (post anesthesia care unit) to be monitored. Guidelines and protocols called "Aldrete scores" exist to protect the patient and make sure that he can breathe on his own (patient is able to breathe unassisted, heart rate and color are okay, and vital signs check out). The anesthesiologist and nurses monitor the patient's vital signs to determine if he can be safely transferred to a medical floor. If the patient has sleep apnea or other respiratory problems, this can complicate the decision surrounding the timing of the patient's release.

- Releasing the patient too early from PACU: In many cases, patients are moved to a medical floor prior to meeting the discharge criteria for PACU. If this happens and the patient is not monitored properly, there can be serious complications.

- Pain management: Anesthesiologists also assist with pain management. In some cases, the injection into the spinal cord, meant for controlling pain, has caused permanent injury.

To their credit, physicians have worked hard to improve the quality of anesthesia care, but it is an area in which a number of different mishaps can occur. Many standards have been issued regarding the administration of different aspects of anesthesia, and there is a wealth of available information on the American Anesthesia Association website, and on my own website (www.mishkindlaw.com), in terms of standards and protocols that must be followed.

Birth defects are the ninth type of medical malpractice. I have handled many birth defect cases, and they are probably the most emotionally charged medical malpractice cases. Imagine being a mother who has followed the doctor's instructions, taken her prenatal vitamins, and attended all of her doctor's appointments. But in some cases, an ultrasound or sonogram was misread so that the anticipated size of the baby was underestimated. As a result, the ability to deliver the baby safely through the vaginal canal is compromised. It is a very scary situation for the parents in the delivery room when this happens, as they watch the entire nursing staff and the obstetrician rushing around, trying to deliver the baby safely.

In these cases, at the time of delivery, too much force may be applied to the baby's head while trying to pull him or her out of the birth canal, since the baby is too large for the birth canal (i.e., shoulder dystocia) or is stuck in the birth canal. Pulling on the baby's head will stretch and injure his or her shoulder nerves, resulting in a brachial plexus injury, or Erb's Palsy—a nerve injury that affects the movement of the baby's shoulders, arms, and hands. Sometimes, a brachial plexus injury is mild, but in severe cases, the nerves are actually torn from the point of attachment to the spine. This can cause the baby to have permanent paralysis of the arms and shoulders, which is devastating to the parents as well as to the child. There are procedures to follow when the projected size of the baby is too large for a normal vaginal birth, and doctors should follow proper guidelines when this occurs, so that the obstetrician and the nursing staff are prepared to put the mother in the best position for delivering the baby. If the guidelines are not followed because the medical staff has panicked, this could lead to serious problems for the mother and child.

There can also be mistakes in reading the fetal monitoring strip when the baby is in distress. The nurses and the obstetrician must monitor the mother's and the baby's vital signs closely, to determine if the baby can be born vaginally or if an emergency C-section must be performed. Problems occur when the fetal heart rate drops into the 80s but does not recover (known as late decelerations).

Another type of injury, cerebral palsy, occurs when there is a lack of oxygen at the time of birth or right after birth. If the baby is unable to breathe on his own, he needs to be given to the neonatal team immediately. However, if there is a lapse of time between resuscitating the baby or in getting the neonatal team into the room, the baby can suffer permanent trauma due to the lack of oxygen.

In each of these situations, the nurses and the obstetrician must communicate well so that the baby is delivered in the safest manner to avoid shoulder dystocia, Erb's Palsy, lack of oxygen, or an infection. All of these situations must be anticipated so that the medical staff can prepare in case of a problem.

All of these injuries are devastating, life-changing injuries for the child. In cases when there is failure to deliver or resuscitate the baby quickly, the family is faced not only with the emotional impact of the situation, but also with the huge economic burden of a lifetime of medical and specialized care for the child. If the doctor is not held accountable and forced to pay, the parents and the baby typically have to turn to Medicaid and public assistance to take care of their needs. The follow-up questions hinge on responsibility: "Should the doctor be held responsible for the medical mistake that caused the brain injury or the trauma? Or should the hospital without the proper system to handle this delivery safely be held responsible? Or should the public, through Medicaid, be the ones to bear the burden?"

These cases require detailed evaluation of the events leading up to the delivery, the delivery itself, and the interventions after the delivery. Attorneys need to obtain the head films, a CAT scan, or an MRI, to show the cause of the baby's paralysis, cerebral palsy, or other injury. Review of blood gases and other factors go into the evaluation of a birth injury claim.

The issue of informed consent is another type of claim frequently found in medical malpractice cases. Before a patient goes in for surgery, the hospital will present the patient with a consent form that must be signed, stating that the patient "consents to the surgery and understands the potential risks." It is presumed that if the patient signs the consent form—provided that the consent form complies with state law—then the patient is absolving the hospital for liability if a complication (i.e., infection, bleeding, paralysis, etc.) occurs as a result of the surgery. However, consent forms or consent to surgery does not mean that the doctor will not and cannot be held legally responsible for a negligence-related complication. The doctor cannot appear in court and wave the consent form as a defense, claiming, "The patient died but he signed the consent form saying that he could die," or "The patient had a stroke but he signed a consent form acknowledging that there was a risk of stroke." If it's proven that the death or the injury was due to negligence and not due to "one of those things that happen, even under the best of circumstances," the consent form is not a get-out-of-jail free card for the doctor.

In Ohio and in other states, a lack of informed consent is another form of a medical claim (in our list, the eleventh type). A doctor must be found to willingly testify regarding the reasonable risks and complications of the procedure, to establish whether or not those reasonable risks were explained to the patient. A reasonable complication is one in which the complications were reasonably explained to the patient, and the patient cannot prove that the doctor was negligent. In this case, the patient has no claim because there is no lack of informed consent.

In some cases, the doctor may perform procedures that are beyond the scope of the consent form, or the doctor did something during surgery without the patient's prior consent. For example, if a doctor is given consent to do an operation on a patient's hand to fix a bone, but decides during the procedure that he is also going to conduct a procedure that is not an emergency (such as repairing a tendon, artery, or ligament). This is not a lack of informed consent: it is medical battery. Medical battery is an unlawful touching of another person—just like assault and battery between two individuals—and damages can be recovered for the unlawful touching. In Ohio, you may be entitled to recover punitive damages to punish and deter such conduct in the future.

Since informed consent cases have different rules, it is important to consult with a qualified and experienced medical malpractice attorney. An attorney can determine whether or not written, informed consent was required, whether that consent is sufficient to protect the hospital or the doctor, and whether or not the doctor exceeded the consent, thus constituting medical battery.

In general, the medical profession has many guidelines and standards that should be followed in the treatment and care of patients, and preventive medical care is critical in these areas. Attorneys see potential medical malpractice claims in all areas: from general medicine to the medical specialists themselves. Patients get injured when corners are cut, or when doctors (for whatever reason) fail to order the required medical tests to accurately diagnose a medical condition. In all cases, attorneys must analyze the case in terms of whether or not the outcome could have been prevented. Unfortunately, we see the same medical errors on a repetitive basis in our office and in other malpractice firms. However, it is important to keep in mind that medical negligence is not a crime. The doctor will not lose his license or go to jail. It is an injury caused by a medical mistake in the care.

PROCEDURAL REQUIREMENTS

In Ohio, as in most states, both medical malpractice cases and medical negligence claims have special rules that set them apart from other personal injury cases. For example, an expert witness, usually another doctor, must testify as to the basis of the claim. He must testify as to what the standard of care was and whether the doctor violated the standard of care and whether the violation was a proximate cause of the injury. In some states, the doctor that is serving as the expert must be from the same state or an adjoining state. In some states, the case has to be submitted to a medical review panel before the case can be filed. In most states, the lawsuit must contain specific information and proof from the beginning otherwise the lawsuit or "complaint" will be dismissed. In an automobile accident case, expert testimony is rarely required to prove negligence at trial. In a medical malpractice case, expert testimony is necessary to allow the jury to understand the technical elements and make a proper determination as to negligence. If the required elements are not established through expert testimony, the case never goes before the jury. For this reason, medical malpractice cases are very expensive in terms of the investigation and prosecution.

In addition, the statute of limitations—the period of time allowed to pursue a medical malpractice case—is different from the statute of limitations for an automobile accident. In Ohio, the statute of limitations for an automobile collision is two years. A medical malpractice case in Ohio has a one-year statute of limitations, generally beginning from the date of the medical event, the termination of the doctor–patient relationship for that event, or the discovery of the injury. This can create a legal nightmare in determining when the one-year stopwatch begins to run.

In Ohio, there is a four-year statute of repose. This means that if a patient continues to go to a doctor after an injury occurs, because he believes the doctor can help him get better and he wants to give the doctor a chance, he only has four years from the date of the injury to realize that he is not getting better and must take legal action. Likewise, if a patient is being treated for a condition but the doctor failed to correctly diagnose the illness, the patient only has four years from the day of the negligent act to take legal action. Claims regarding babies vary depending on the state. In Ohio, if a baby is injured, the statute of limitations begins to run on his or her 18th birthday.

EXPERT REQUIREMENTS

As discussed previously, it is essential for the patient to have an expert witness to testify to the elements of the case. In Ohio, that expert must meet certain requirements to qualify as an expert witness. The witness cannot be retired and must currently spend a certain amount of professional time in the active clinical practice of medicine. The requirements for expert witnesses vary from state to state. Some states allow expert witnesses to testify even though they are retired but may require all experts to be from that state or an adjoining state. I can analyze the medical care for individuals throughout the country, but in terms of handling a case, most states have their own specific rules that must be applied.

Before you can file a medical malpractice lawsuit in Ohio, unlike in an automobile accident case, an expert witness must sign an affidavit of merit, stating that there is validity to the claim. The elements of a medical malpractice case are fairly simple to define: duty and breach of the standards of care. The physician has a legally recognized duty to the patient, and this duty is created by the physician–patient relationship. That requires the physician to act in accordance with specific norms or standards established by the profession rather than standards established by everyday members of society. The medical community determines the standards of what is reasonable and prudent. That is what separates medical malpractice cases from other personal injury cases. You must have an expert witness to testify, "The standard of care and the obligation of the doctor was to do X, Y, and Z." Without an expert witness to clearly state the standard of care, the case cannot be won, no matter how terrible the injury was for the patient.

After proving what was the standard of care, it must then be proven that there was a breach of that standard of care. The patient must show that the physician failed to act in accordance with the standards through either an act or an omission. In other words, the doctor did, or failed to do, something that differed from what a "reasonable" doctor under like or similar circumstances would have done.

Lastly, causation must be proven: The patient must show a connection between the act—or omission of action—by the doctor and the resulting injury. Again, sometimes a bad result or injury occurs, and there may be an act of negligence or breach in the standard of care, but an attorney cannot prove that the act or negligence was the legal cause of the injury. All of these issues must be established in order to have a basis for a medical malpractice case, and the key is an expert witness.

Patients should not panic out of the fear of being the next victim of medical error, even after reviewing common types of medical malpractice and the rules of pursuing possible claims. In most cases, patients receive high-quality medical care and doctors want to help their patients to heal. However, according to statistics published in the Institute of Medicine's 2000 publication, "To Err is Human: Building a Safer Health System," medical errors kill up to 98,000 Americans each year. Recent studies have shown that the number of deaths from medical mistakes may be four times the number previously reported, or as high as 440,000 deaths each year. Unfortunately and frustratingly, in the United States, a safer health system does not appear to have occurred in our culture and society.

In addition to deaths, countless preventable injuries occur each year due to medical mistakes. Many of these patients are silent victims whose claims cannot be pursued by attorneys, due to certain limits enacted by various state legislatures. Even if the cases are pursued, the average juror is still likely to find a way to excuse a doctor or a hospital when the case goes to trial, thinking, "If I had been that patient, I would have done more and would have never allowed that injury to happen to me."

That type of thought process has made it more difficult for injured victims of medical errors to receive proper compensation and care. My hope is that, in the future, hospitals and healthcare organizations will put patients before profits and prioritize patient safety measures, so that damaging and life-threatening medical errors and complications will decrease rather than increase. That is ultimately the aim of anyone involved in the work of a medical malpractice attorney. After more than 34 years of representing victims of medical errors and continuing to see an increasing number of reports that our healthcare system is broken and that patient safety seems to be a hot topic but not a topic that is being fixed, it is frustrating.

I truly believe we have some of the finest doctors and hospitals in the world, but the measures that are being taken to keep patients safe are failing at an alarming rate and too many innocent patients are being hurt rather than helped by medical care. I view myself more as a medical safety advocate but until systems are set up to prevent near misses and catastrophes in healthcare, there will always be a need to hold those that make avoidable mistakes accountable. I hope that this chapter opens your eyes to the truth about medical care and that there truly is too much medical malpractice and far too few medical claims being filed and compensation awarded. In fact, due to laws passed that harm and limit patients' rights, the number of legitimate claims have dropped throughout the country. More and more individuals that placed their trust in their doctors are winding up injured and under- or un-compensated due to the laws that place limits on what can be awarded by a jury in a medical malpractice action.

The number of people that suffer injury in hospitals and doctors' offices that go uncompensated is tremendous, and in most cases, the compensation awarded by a jury is insufficient to right the wrong. Most people would rather turn the hands of the clock back to before the injury was caused, but that can't happen.

In conclusion, to the true heroes (the skilled attorneys that represent victims of medical mistakes knowing how difficult it is to prevail) that fight for our clients throughout the country, I salute you and encourage you to keep up the good fight for our neighbors and family members. I hope that the next patient that you represent due to a medical mistake that should not have occurred, will result in changes in healthcare just like the changes that have improved auto safety, product safety, aviation safety, and so much more. If only we could translate those safety measures into a culture where medical injuries and deaths in the hospital and doctors' offices and nursing homes were prevented and profits were invested in increasing the safety of each and every one of us, I would be a happier human being. God Bless.

(This content should be used for informational purposes only. It does not create an attorney-client relationship with any reader and should not be construed as legal advice. If you need legal advice, please contact an attorney in your community who can assess the specifics of your situation.)

4

COMMON CONCERNS IF YOU ARE IN A SERIOUS ACCIDENT

by Jonathan S. Safran, Esq.

Jonathan S. Safran, Esq.
Samster, Konkel & Safran, S.C.
Milwaukee, Wisconsin

Jonathan S. Safran is a founding member and a shareholder in the firm of Samster, Konkel & Safran, S.C. He is a 1983 graduate of Indiana University at Bloomington School of Law. He has been practicing personal injury law in Milwaukee for more than twenty-five years.

He is committed to helping clients put their lives back together after a serious accident. He seeks justice and a fair settlement for each client and understands the importance of staying in touch with each victim and communicating the progress of one's claim as it goes through the claims and legal processes.

He is actively involved in civic organizations, serving on national and local boards of the Arthritis Foundation, the Board of the YMCA of Metropolitan Milwaukee, Camp Matawa, and the Mequon-Thiensville Chamber of Commerce Board of Directors.

COMMON CONCERNS IF YOU ARE IN A SERIOUS ACCIDENT

I believe that it is important for people to contact an experienced personal injury attorney whenever they are injured in an accident. Most people do not know what to expect when they speak to an attorney and they usually have numerous questions about the claims process. The following are common concerns that individuals have when they call or see me to discuss a vehicle accident:

- How do I get a rental car if my vehicle is not drivable or is being repaired?
- How will I get to my doctor's visits?
- What should I do about my job?
- How will I pay my bills if my injuries prevent me from working?
- Who will be responsible for obtaining copies of my medical records?
- How long does it take for my case to be completed?

Experienced personal injury attorneys understand their clients' needs, respond to their clients' worries so as to alleviate their anxieties, and address the previous concerns and other issues in a timely manner. That is why it is so important for an injured person to contact a personal injury attorney right away. The injured person can then concentrate on receiving medical care and making a full recovery, and the personal injury attorney can assist the client with his or her immediate concerns while also handling the many legal matters: investigating the accident, obtaining evidence, and contacting witnesses; filing the claims with the identified insurance companies; assisting to resolve the client's property damage; obtaining required medical records and documentation; investigating the best ways to maximize recovery of the client's losses; keeping the client informed of the claims process; and keeping the insurance companies from taking advantage of the situation, etc.

Since many individuals will hopefully only deal with one serious injury caused by an accident during their lifetime, the process is unfamiliar to them. Many individuals are embarrassed when they call me and say, "This is just not me. I don't like to talk to attorneys or sue people or cause trouble." When I encounter this situation, I begin by explaining the overall process to help them feel at ease.

First, I want them to understand that talking to me does not cost them anything, and I encourage them to ask me as many questions as they like. I am happy to give them as much free information and free advice during the initial telephone call or consultation as they desire. Since 90–95% of our cases are resolved without the necessity of filing a lawsuit, I let them know that it is often not required that we file a lawsuit and name them as a party to sue another person: we, on their behalf, are simply attempting to settle their claims at the claims-stage of the process, without any litigation being necessary.

Second—as I tell people who contact me—my law firm usually assists clients in receiving full compensation for their injuries and damages from the insurance company of the at-fault person. The person responsible for the accident and their injuries has paid an insurance premium for self-protection. People pay insurance premiums for insurance coverage to protect themselves: if someone is involved in an accident that is his or her fault, insurance is available to pay the party who sustained injuries or damages as a result of the accident. Most people who are at fault in an accident want the accident victim to be fully compensated. The client's claim against the insurance company generally will not further affect the insurance of the person responsible for the accident: the fact that the responsible party caused the accident has usually already set changes in motion in their insurance rates before the injured party even makes a claim. I assure clients that I will not make more out of a claim than they deserve; however, I do want to be certain that I secure all of the compensation they need and deserve, in order to cover the accident-related injuries and damages they sustained, as I attempt to make them "whole" (the term used to describe their condition prior to the accident) again.

It is crucial for injured individuals to obtain all of the medical care that is necessary in order to help their injuries attempt to fully resolve. The process of following up with doctors, therapists, chiropractors, specialists, having tests performed, etc. can almost seem as though it is a full-time job. However, consistent care is crucial, most importantly to help alleviate an individual's pain and injuries, but also to allow the attorney to document the pain and suffering experienced by an accident victim and obtain the maximum claim value to compensate the person. The same can be said about missing time from work following an accident. No one wants to miss time from work and avoid being paid, however, a medical provider may recommend to an injured individual that he or she should not work, if it is felt that the work will aggravate the injuries or prolong the recovery. Experienced personal injury attorneys also realize that it is important for their clients to return to work as soon as possible following an accident, as long as their health care providers approve, so their client will continue to have a steady stream of income to pay bills, resulting in less stress and anxiety. Personal injury attorneys will explain these matters to their clients in order to help them understand the claims process and assure them that their best interests are being looked after.

THE COST TO HIRE A PERSONAL INJURY ATTORNEY

Beyond the fear of speaking with an attorney who they believe to be in possible "lawsuit mode," people are often concerned about the cost of hiring an attorney. Typically, the cost of hiring an attorney is one-third (33 1/3%) of the ultimate recovery; however, it can sometimes be as high as 40%, depending upon the complexity of the case. On rare occasions, if there is an appeal involved from a lawsuit verdict, the percentages can go slightly higher. However, that is always discussed and explained with the potential client. I appreciate that the typical one-third seems like a significant amount, and I understand that injured potential clients want to know the benefit of hiring an attorney versus going through the process alone.

Personal injury attorneys in most states are permitted to work on a "contingency fee basis." This means that a client can hire any attorney he or she wants, usually without paying any up-front fees or costs. With a contingency fee, he does not have to pay any attorney fees until and unless there is a recovery in the case. The attorney fees are then based upon the agreed-upon percentage of the ultimate recovery. A contingency fee allows anyone, regardless of his or her financial state, to hire an experienced personal injury attorney and be provided with the same protection afforded to someone who is very wealthy. It really levels the playing field to ensure that everyone receives the same protection and the best legal representation in a case.

In addition to the attorney fees, which are to compensate the attorney for the time spent by the attorneys and staff on the case, personal injury attorneys, in their retainer agreements or engagement letters, will also explain that clients will be responsible for what are called "costs or disbursements," or out-of-pocket expenses paid by the attorney to someone outside of his law firm for the performance of certain tasks.

For example, we must request medical records for our clients from a hospital, medical office, or medical records service, and they will in turn charge us for providing those records. While the charges are often based upon a per-page rate, there might also be a retrieval fee and postage charges added to that per-page total. Regardless of the price, the attorney will pay those charges because that is what is required to obtain copies of the client's medical records. The same principle applies to the expenses of hiring outside investigators, obtaining accident reports or other police records, hiring expert witnesses, or paying lawsuit-related filing charges, deposition expenses, trial-related costs, and other expenses related to preparing the case for settlement or trial. Careful records are kept of all expenses incurred during the case so that the attorney can be reimbursed from the eventual settlement proceeds. Our clients are generally not required to pay those costs or disbursements as the case progresses; and most experienced attorneys who handle personal injury cases are willing to advance those costs for their clients, with the agreed-upon understanding that the attorneys will be reimbursed for their out-of-pocket costs and disbursements from the eventual settlement proceeds.

THE MONEY YOU LEAVE ON THE TABLE GOES TO THE INSURANCE COMPANY

Once in a while, I run across individuals who tell me that they think they might be able to keep more money if they handle a personal injury case themselves. After more than thirty years of practice, it has been proven to me that when an experienced attorney gets involved in a case, the client is generally able to recover a larger amount than if he or she tried to handle the case on his or her own. Insurance companies understand that when attorneys are involved, there is typically a contingency fee agreement for the fees and costs—this is taken into consideration when an offer is made. More importantly, assuming that the client has an experienced personal injury attorney, the attorney will know how to maximize the value of the injured party's claims, and the attorney will know what needs to be done to get the injured client full compensation for his or her injuries and damages.

My experience has shown that clients who are not represented by attorneys generally do not understand what issues to explore or what they may be fully entitled to receive as part of a settlement. Our law firm has witnessed many situations throughout years of practice where clients have attempted to negotiate their own settlements with insurance companies, only to come to us after they continue to receive very low offers in return. Unfortunately, people can paint themselves into a corner with the insurance company in these situations. Sometimes, when individuals contact me after they have been involved in negotiations on their own, I have to tell them that hiring me may not be in their best interest. If the value of the claim is actually higher than the amount the individual has requested, I have to explain to him that we have lost any negotiating power we might have previously had. Sometimes my ability to negotiate has been limited by what the individual has already done in his case, such as by his speaking with the insurance company adjuster or by providing the insurance company with information or documents.

In many cases, the client has already provided information to the insurance company prior to meeting with an attorney. As an example, we often find that insurance companies will contact individuals shortly after an accident and obtain recorded statements from them. In these statements, the individual has often agreed on the record that any statements he or she makes could be used in a court of law. While individuals believe they are being cooperative and telling the truth, insurance company adjusters will sometimes ask questions that will instigate a response from individuals that will hurt their case and help the insurance company.

Many states, including Wisconsin, have the legal principle known as "comparative negligence." This legal theory means that more than one individual may be found to be partially negligent in an accident. When obtaining a statement, the insurance adjuster's questions will often elicit information to help establish comparative negligence and increase the percentage of the injured individual's responsibility. For instance, in a vehicle collision, the adjuster may ask the injured individual who was driving if he or she saw the other vehicle before the collision. Often, individuals may say that they did not see the other vehicle until right before the collision happened. The adjuster may use this response to portray the individual as being inattentive or distracted at the time of the collision. The same concern occurs if the adjuster should ask what the individual did in an attempt to avoid the collision. With a typical response such as "it happened so fast that I did not have a chance to do anything," this will often be construed as an admission that the individual was not properly controlling his or her vehicle. These types of issues and responses can increase the percentage of comparative negligence and reduce the value of the injured person's claim, because the settlement amount will be reduced by the percentage of comparative negligence assessed to the individual. These are examples of reasons why an insurance company will want to get a statement from an injured party before the individual has an opportunity to speak with an attorney, and demonstrate why people need to consult with a personal injury attorney as early as possible.

Since experienced personal injury attorneys are routinely involved in negotiating settlements, mediating cases, and trying cases before a judge or a jury, we have a better understanding of the value of claims. Many of us are also involved in state and national trial lawyer organizations which monitor settlements and trial verdicts, allowing us even more information as to case values. Therefore, we can provide guidance to an injured individual by helping him or her receive proper and maximum compensation for his or her injuries and damages. It is very difficult for individuals to present a claim themselves and receive the full value of the claim; especially after negotiations have dragged along, and the individuals have already discussed with the insurance company their ideas on the value of their claims and possible settlement amounts. This can make the situation more difficult, as opposed to if the injured party were to contact an attorney as soon as possible after an accident.

The simple fact is this: my experience has shown that I am generally able to obtain greater compensation for my clients than they are able to obtain on their own. When we meet for the first time and an individual expresses the concern that she might receive less compensation due to hiring and paying the fees and costs to me and my law firm, I explain the reasons and the specific situations that would allow me to pursue a larger amount for them and to maximize her net recovery. Usually, this relieves her concerns about hiring me and my law firm as her attorneys.

As an experienced personal injury attorney, I want to do everything possible to ensure that our client's lost wages are recovered, that all bills are paid, and that any out-of-pocket expenses are reimbursed. As a compassionate personal injury attorney, my goal is to also help our clients achieve the best possible recovery, while having them regain a state of health as similar as possible to their pre-accident condition, and allowing them to move forward and return to "normalcy" in their lives. I discuss with the client that her case will eventually end, but life will go on, so their job is to focus on obtaining appropriate medical care, and let me and my staff take care of the legal issues and other tasks relating to their claims.

THE INSURANCE COMPANY IS NOT YOUR FRIEND, THEY ARE YOUR ADVERSARY

When a client retains a personal injury attorney, it is imperative that there be opportunities for the client to speak with the attorney himself and not just with members of his staff. Personal injury law is a very specialized area of the law; therefore, the attorney should be actively involved throughout the course of the entire case, and should have all of the necessary education, training, and experience needed in order to assist in the claim. The client and the attorney should have a good working relationship so they can collaborate as a team: this is a very important element in reaching a satisfactory outcome. A client should feel comfortable with the attorney's level of knowledge, the attorney should be compassionate in understanding the client's struggles and concerns, and the client should be satisfied that the attorney is keeping him or her informed as the case progresses.

When I am retained by a client in a personal injury case, my first steps are to obtain a detailed description of the incident, a detailed history of his injuries and treatment to-date, and then answer any questions the client might have. I will then notify the insurance company of my representation of the injured party. My office staff and I then attempt to assist the client with his property damage claims, such as the repair or replacement of his vehicle, in addition to assisting him in obtaining a rental vehicle for use while his vehicle is being appraised or repaired. After the insurance company has been notified of my involvement, insurance representatives should not contact my clients directly, as all communication should take place through my office only.

Most insurance companies will require certain information in order to adequately evaluate a claim: information about the circumstances surrounding the accident's occurrence, what my client was doing when the accident occurred, the severity of my client's injuries, whether my client had relevant prior medical conditions, the treatment which my client has received, and whether my client is employed and missing time from work. My staff and I work to obtain this information, along with the necessary medical records, proof of lost wages, documentation of out-of-pocket expenses, and any other information required by the insurance company for their claim evaluation. As the personal injury case progresses, we continually communicate with the insurance company adjuster so that the insurance company is informed about the progress of the client's injury treatment and recovery, and his or her work status. This information and medical documentation is provided to allow the adjuster to review the case file and so that the insurance company has the ability to set aside sufficient reserves (money) to pay the claim, once we reach the point of discussing settlement.

Of course, after each document is obtained, we review it for accuracy and completion, prior to providing the information to the insurance company. Once the insurance company has all of the necessary documentation to substantiate and establish my client's losses, we negotiate with the insurance company to insure that our clients are reimbursed fully for all expenses, lost income, and damages related to the injuries sustained in the accident. In every personal injury case, we strive to settle cases so that our clients are made "whole," in order to allow them to continue with their lives, hopefully without lingering problems, and to be assured that they are fully compensated for their losses. It is well recognized that the length of time it takes for individuals to recover from injuries will differ from one person to another. Experienced personal injury attorneys will not attempt to settle an injury claim until either the client is discharged from treatment as being fully re-covered, or the client's health care provider has determined that he or she has reached a healing plateau, but has sustained some level of permanent injury.

Many personal injury cases have multiple insurance companies involved. Once retained by a client, one of our law firm's initial steps is to identify all possible liable parties and all possible insurance companies that may potentially be held responsible for paying claim damages. Depending upon the type of personal injury case, some insurance companies will require different information to evaluate the claim than others. For example, if the injury is work-related, a worker's compensation insurance company may need specific information that would not be required by a liability insurance company. Since we know what is required by the different insurance companies in each different situation, we will quickly provide the required documentation so that each insurance company can complete its investigation and be prepared to negotiate an appropriate resolution of the case.

Some insurance companies have the right to obtain statements from our clients, while others do not. Depending on the type of case, the client's own insurance company (or often a Workers' Compensation insurance company) may or may not have the right to obtain a statement. However, if the client's own insurance company is involved and they claim to be entitled to obtain certain information mandated by the insurance policy, the client's experienced personal injury attorney will determine how the client needs to respond and will then assist the client in preparing and providing the information. The attorney should also be present with the client if he or she is required to provide any such information to the insurance company in person. Experienced personal injury attorneys will determine whether an insurance company will have a right to request and obtain certain documents as part of the claims process.

Injured individuals must understand one thing: insurance companies are not their friends. Insurance companies are in business to make a profit. The insurance company claims adjuster's job is to minimize the amount they must pay to an injured individual. In order to do this, they will often try to settle a claim as quickly as they can and for as little compensation as possible in order to prevent claims from increasing over time. In some situations—especially if the individual does not yet have an attorney—the insurance company may offer an inappropriately small sum, for the amount of damages that have been (or will be) suffered by the injured person. In the early stages of a personal injury case, the value of the case is often not really well known: neither by the individual nor the attorney nor the insurance company. Many factors must be considered when determining the value of a personal injury case: the circumstances of the accident, the mechanism of the injury's occurrence, the type of treatment obtained, the length of treatment for the injuries sustained, the amount of any lost wages or income, the possibility of disfigurement or permanent injury, the potential and cost of future treatment, and the expectation of any future lost wages, income, or loss of future earning capacity.

Experienced personal injury attorneys understand what needs to be done to fully investigate an accident and maximize the client's chances for a full recovery. A few years ago, I was retained in a case involving a young boy who was severely injured while he was running across the street. As he was running—outside of the crosswalk—he was struck by a vehicle and suffered significant leg and head injuries. The driver hit the boy without braking, and the driver claimed that he was not able to see the boy before striking him with his vehicle. Even though the police report showed that other vehicles and witnesses were nearby, the police did not obtain complete information from the witnesses to determine all of the facts relevant to the collision. The insurance company denied the claim, alleging that the boy ran into the street in front of the car, that he was the majority at fault, and that the driver was not able to avoid the collision.

When my law firm got involved in the case, we fully reviewed the accident report and then contacted witnesses: most importantly, the driver of a second vehicle, just behind the vehicle that struck our client. As he was driving down the road, that witness told us that he could see this young boy on the sidewalk, and it appeared to him as though the boy was about to run across the street. Though the witness was a good distance away, he started to brake because he was concerned about the boy's potential actions. From this witness' statement and testimony, we were able to establish that he was certainly able to observe the boy and slow down, in an attempt to avoid potentially striking the child. This, in turn, helped us to establish that the driver of the vehicle that struck our client was not paying sufficient attention and that he made no attempt to avoid striking our client.

When discussing the complexity of the claims process, I stress this point to my clients: "If the insurance companies were fair and reasonable, you would be able to submit information to them so that they could evaluate your claim, and they would pay you a fair-value settlement." If this scenario was true, no personal injury attorney would be needed to assist with any claim. However, that is just not a reflection of the real world. I am not implying that insurance company claims adjusters are bad people. Simply said, insurance company adjusters are fully trained in the fact that insurance companies are in business to make profits, and they are, therefore, encouraged to minimize or avoid claim payments. Due to the insurance company adjusters' training, it is important to have an experienced personal injury attorney retained to make sure that an injured person receives the full value of deserved compensation.

Another concerning issue which occurs in personal injury cases is that frequently insurance company adjusters will tell an injured individual that a blank authorization form is needed so the insurance company can obtain copies of the injured party's medical records and establish the person's injuries, damages, and the treatment received. With a signed blank authorization form, the insurance company has the ability to receive any medical record for the injured individual, and often for any time period. Experienced personal injury attorneys are very careful with what we allow our clients to sign; however, individuals dealing directly with the insurance company are often only trying to be cooperative when they sign the requested forms, believing that the forms will be used appropriately. They are not thinking that the insurance company will use these forms for any other purpose than to receive medical records generated due to accident-related injuries and treatment. The problem is that many people have other medical conditions, having nothing to do with injuries sustained in the accident, such as arthritis, fibromyalgia, or prior temporary injuries, which the insurance company may use as a reason to reduce the value of the claim. Often, when we meet with an injured individual, they do not even recall prior medical issues or treatment—such as a few visits to a chiropractor for temporary neck stiffness— because they are only thinking about their current injuries.

Unfortunately, once a blank medical authorization form has been signed by the injured party and given to the insurance company, the attorney and the client will not know what the insurance company has obtained and discovered, until the insurance company potentially makes the argument that a pre-existing medical condition is the partial or sole cause of the client's post-accident medical condition and treatment.

COMMON LANDMINES TO AVOID

Strict notice deadlines are another common problem area with some personal injury claims. This situation often occurs when a governmental agency is involved in the personal injury case, such as a vehicle accident with a transit company bus, fire truck, or police car, or if a person falls on a city sidewalk. In these cases, very strict notice requirements must be met for a claim to be pursued. As an example, in Wisconsin, when a governmental entity or its employee is involved in causing an accident and injury, only 120 days are often allowed for the injured individual to file the required notice document with the proper governmental office or employee, which notifies the governmental agency of a potential future claim for damages. If that notice document is not completed properly, filed properly, or notice is not provided in a timely manner, those errors might affect the ability to have the claim pursued and eventually successfully resolved. Unfortunately, many people do not know about these notice requirements. When our law firm receives a call several months after an accident, and I determine that a governmental entity is involved, I ask if the individual has filed the required notice form. Unfortunately, there have been too many times when the injured caller had no idea that such a form needed to be filed, and that failure to have filed the notice form may have extinguished the claim.

In addition to notice forms involving governmental entities, each state and jurisdiction has a "statute of limitations"—deadlines by which a claim must be settled or a lawsuit must be filed—often different time deadlines depending upon the type of claim. Insurance companies often do not advise people of these deadlines. In several situations over the years, individuals have contacted me for help either right before, or even after, the statute of limitations time period has expired. Unfortunately, in situations where the time period has expired, I am not able to help them because it is too late to pursue a claim.

The same issue emerges with automobile insurance policies and situations involving medical bills which must be submitted to the policyholder's insurance company within a specified period of time. Most people do not read their insurance policies, and most insurance companies do not explain these time periods to their customers. That is just one more reason to involve an experienced personal injury attorney, who will not allow time periods to expire, or a claim to be extinguished.

Settlement documents bring up additional issues, because they are agreements as well as contracts. Sometimes, insurance companies will knowingly ask a client to sign a document that may affect the future of the case and other claims. I have seen situations where injured individuals were presented with an offer to settle their vehicle damage. However, the settlement release document contained language specifying that the injured party was agreeing to accept the money for all personal injuries and other types of claims, in addition to the agreed-upon property damage claim settlement. Once signed, a release form is a binding contract. The language included in a release form may prevent the injured person from pursuing other claims related to an accident.

This situation also occurs sometimes when an adverse liability insurance company offers the full policy limit of its coverage to settle its liability for a claim. If the correct release form is not used, if other applicable insurance companies are not provided sufficient notice, or if the release form contains specific language that releases all insurance companies, the injured person might be prevented from pursuing other claims, such as for underinsured motorist coverage against his or her own automobile insurance policy. Therefore, it is very important to consult with an experienced personal injury attorney prior to signing any release form or other documents. The attorney should review the documents to determine that the language does not preclude or have a negative impact on future claims that the injured party may still wish to pursue.

SUBROGATION RIGHTS OF INSURANCE COMPANIES

In most personal injury cases, the claims involve not only others' liability insurance companies, but also the injured person's own health insurance company, and in automobile accident cases, often his own automobile insurance company. When pursuing a personal injury case, we explain to our clients that their health insurance company, and potentially their own automobile insurance company, pursuant to any medical expense coverage or personal injury protection insurance coverage, usually have what is known as "subrogation" rights. That means that each insurance company often has the right to be reimbursed, from the client's eventual settlement proceeds, for accident-related costs and expenses that were paid by the insurance company and utilized as part of the liability injury claim.

There are often exceptions to this general subrogation and reimbursement rule. Under some state laws, the health insurance company's or automobile insurance company's right of recovery depends upon whether or not the injured person has been "made whole" from the liability insurance settlement. In many situations, we have been able to convince the client's health insurance company and the client's automobile insurance company that they should waive their reimbursement claims completely or be bound to reduce their claim and accept the percentage of comparative negligence attributed to our client, so that the health insurance company or automobile insurance company only receives reimbursement of a lesser percentage (rather than 100%) of its payments. This reduction can be attributed to liability comparisons or the fact that our client has not been made whole from the ultimate liability settlement. In other situations, the insurance company will agree to accept a reduction in order to pay towards a portion of the injured client's attorney's fees and costs because we have assisted the insurance company to recover some or all of its payments, even though we are not working directly for them.

As an experienced personal injury attorney, I work all available avenues in order to maximize the net financial recovery for our clients. I will pursue the insurance companies that are liable to assure that they pay the maximum amount of damages to our client, as well as negotiate with health insurance companies or others who have paid our client's medical bills in order to lower the subrogation amounts that must be paid back as reimbursement for those medical payments. By combining all of these strategies, more money goes to our clients.

Even though we must identify all subrogation rights, many individuals do not realize that these subrogation rights are often negotiable, even when paid by governmental entities. The Federal Medicare program, for example, has a "super right" of recovery. Liability insurance companies are now required to identify whether someone is receiving or is eligible to receive Medicare benefits. As a result of this situation, insurance companies must now contact Medicare to confirm benefits and the amount, if any, paid on behalf of covered individuals. If Medicare has paid medical benefits related to an accident claim, the payments must be protected as part of the settlement. Potentially, the client, the client's attorney, and the liability insurance company can be held liable for having to reimburse Medicare if its subrogation or reimbursement claim is not taken into consideration as part of the eventual injury settlement. The same is true if a client is receiving a State health insurance provided program benefit. They also must generally be notified of a client's claim, and an experienced personal injury attorney may be able to work with them in an attempt to negotiate a reduction of their subrogation or reimbursement claim at the end of the case.

Experienced personal injury attorneys will ensure that Medicare is immediately notified of a client's personal injury claim, if there is the potential that Medicare may make medical payments. There can often be long delays in getting information from Medicare. Therefore, it is imperative that they be notified as early as possible and that we obtain updated payment information from them as the case progresses. At the end of the case, experienced attorneys should be able to obtain a reduction of Medicare's reimbursement claim based upon a Medicare formula that applies in these types of situations.

Medicare reimbursement claims have become much more complicated over the last few years. In some case situations, there is the potential for a "Medicare set-aside," especially in cases which involve a permanent injury that will require ongoing future medical treatment, requiring a fixed amount of money being set aside from the settlement proceeds to be used in lieu of Medicare making payment for those future medical bills. Experienced personal injury attorneys understand that this situation needs to be properly addressed, and we often work with outside companies to arrange for the minimum necessary Medicare set-aside plans. It is our goal to make sure that we protect our clients, while we maximize their settlement recovery. We also want to make sure that, as they continue to age, our clients have the ability to receive future Medicare benefits to cover their medical expenses.

In some cases, the party who caused a vehicle collision may not have any liability insurance. (Luckily, this is less frequent, as most states now have mandatory insurance requirements.) Even though states may have mandatory automobile liability insurance coverage requirements, unfortunately, our firm still sees cases where a party is injured due to the fault of another and the at-fault party has no liability insurance coverage. In automobile collisions, in most states where the responsible party does not have liability insurance but the injured party or the injured party's family members have automobile insurance, there is usually the ability to make claims under what is called Uninsured Motorist Coverage. In Wisconsin, as in many other states, Uninsured Motorist Coverage is considered "personal and portable," meaning that it goes with you and covers you in many types of vehicle-related accidents. An example is where a pedestrian is struck by a vehicle that is not covered by a vehicle liability insurance policy, however, the pedestrian may still be covered by the pedestrian's or pedestrian's family's automobile insurance coverage, even though he or she was not in a vehicle at the time of the collision. The same situation may apply when someone is riding a bicycle and he or she is injured by an uninsured motor vehicle.

In situations where I discover that the responsible person for a vehicle collision did not have liability insurance, it is very important that I uncover whether or not the injured person or a member of his or her household has any liability insurance coverage on any owned vehicles. We have had many situations when the responsible party does not have insurance coverage, and we have been able to assist our client in obtaining compensation under his or her own automobile insurance policy, the insurance policy of a family member, or sometimes even under the insurance policy of an unrelated resident in that household.

When in an accident, most clients are rightfully concerned about the payment of their medical bills. Many assume that the insurance company for the responsible driver will take on that responsibility and pay the medical bills as they are incurred and as the case proceeds. Hopefully, the insurance company for the responsible party will eventually pay the medical bills, plus the value of the claim, at the time of the ultimate settlement. Unfortunately, for several reasons, medical bill or wage loss payments are typically not paid until a settlement is ultimately reached.

First, most liability insurance companies are not equipped to pay medical bills as each bill is incurred. Second, many insurance companies do not want their payment of bills or lost wages to be construed as an acceptance that the medical care and treatment, or missed time from work, was reasonable; or that the medical care, medical bills, or missed time from work were necessarily caused by the accident, until settlement negotiations occur. However, the biggest reason for insurance companies not paying medical bills or wage losses as they are incurred is that these payments might be argued to extend the deadline of the statute of limitations time period. By law, the time periods in statutes of limitations are there in essence to protect insurance companies from parties waiting years to file a claim and expecting payment.

Although the injured party may usually desire that the liability insurance company pay the medical bills as they become due, this rarely happens. Therefore, I encourage my clients to first use their health insurance, if they have the available insurance coverage, to cover medical expenses. If they are involved in a vehicle accident, I also contact my client's own vehicle insurance company to determine if they have medical expense coverage available under their policy. That coverage can be used, up to the policy limit of such coverage, to pay outstanding medical bills, usually after the health insurance company has paid its share of the bills. As the case proceeds, I attempt to use any available vehicle medical expense coverage to reimburse my clients for medical bills they may have paid already, or to pay my clients' outstanding co-pays or deductibles incurred pursuant to their health insurance coverage. This process generally works to avoid the necessity of my clients having to incur out-of-pocket payments for their medical expenses. My office assists clients in sending their outstanding bills to their auto insurance company for payment, pursuant to the medical expense coverage available under their auto insurance policy.

In one situation, I represented an individual who was a passenger in the vehicle of an intoxicated driver who caused a one-vehicle collision. Unfortunately, in the vehicle collision my client sustained very serious injuries. My client had health insurance and owned his own business. His own personal vehicle was actually a company-owned vehicle with significant insurance coverage limits. Living at home, his household included both his parents and his brother, and each owned a separate vehicle which was covered by a separate vehicle liability insurance policy. Due to the serious nature of my client's injuries, he incurred significant medical bills and he had limited health insurance coverage with a high deductible and numerous co-pays. Our law firm contacted all available insurance companies to have claims established and then we worked with the client by submitting his outstanding medical bills: first to his health insurance carrier, second to his own vehicle insurance company's medical expense coverage, third to his parent's vehicle insurance company's medical expense coverage (since he lived with them), and finally to his brother's vehicle insurance company's medical expense coverage. (Again, he lived in the same household with a separately insured vehicle and insurance policy.)

In this case, my client had hundreds of thousands of dollars in medical expenses which were all paid by using a combination of health insurance and automobile insurance policies in the household. Again, even though the responsible vehicle liability insurance company was not paying the medical bills as they were incurred, my client also did not have to pay any medical bills himself, and this was a good example of the principle that there are often other ways for the bills to be paid, if you have an experienced personal injury attorney and office staff involved in your personal injury case.

It is always my goal to limit what clients pay out-of-pocket for their medical expenses in a way that protects them. I want my clients to concentrate on their medical care and their recovery, and avoid the concern with outstanding medical bills. Coordination is needed to make sure that the bills are being properly processed and paid, so as to avoid additional client stress, and to maximize the client's recovery. It is also necessary to ensure that the client is not having their credit affected negatively by medical bills remaining outstanding or being sent to collection agencies for recovery or possible lawsuits.

DISTRACTED DRIVERS CAUSE MOST ACCIDENTS

Obviously, one of the most effective ways to avoid the financial difficulties which follow accidents with injuries is simply this: focus attention on the prevention of accidents. My law firm sees an increasing number of automobile collisions which involve distracted drivers. It is my belief that this trend will continue because of the frequent use of cell phones while driving, and the increasing number of vehicles that are equipped with all types of distracting electronic devices. I have seen this phenomenon myself in two of my own personal vehicle collisions, the first was where my vehicle was rear-ended by a driver who was trying to replace his coffee cup into the cup holder and was not paying attention to my car and the two cars in front of me who were stopped at a stop light. In the second situation, I was rear-ended by the driver of a delivery truck who was apparently distracted while making a turn and did not notice that I had stopped in front of him due to my yielding to oncoming traffic, before pulling forward.

In the split seconds when each driver took his eyes off the road, they each rear-ended me, with the first of the collisions involving damage and injuries to me and my vehicle, as well as the drivers and the two vehicles in front of me, as my vehicle was pushed forward and caused to collide with both vehicles ahead of me. In the second collision, ironically while on my way to give a distracted driving presentation at a local high school, I suffered slight injuries, but sustained significant damage to the rear of my vehicle.

Due to the significant increase in the number of vehicle collisions caused by texting while driving and other distracted driving activities, our law firm is actively involved in speaking at schools, driving school classes, and civic organizations, while also participating in public service announcements to alert people to the risk involved in these types of situations. Our law firm has found that almost 25% of all vehicle collisions involve people—both teens and adults—who were either texting while driving or distracted in another way that decreased their driving ability and led to the collision. When you are texting while driving, statistics show that your eyes leave the road for an average of 4.6 seconds. The mathematics proves that if you are driving at 55 miles per hour on a highway and your eyes leave the road for almost five seconds, you are traveling approximately the length of a football field without looking at the road. One can only imagine the types of accidents that can occur when your car is traveling 100 yards without anyone in control, because you are not looking where you are going.

Even though it would seem to be common sense not to drive while you are distracted, people often feel that doing more than one thing at a time is the best way to proceed through their day. However, this multi-tasking mentality is leading to an increased number of accidents, injuries and deaths on the roadway. More agencies and companies need to spread the word that distracted driving is a very dangerous behavior, and that it can lead to the distracted drivers, their friends, their co-workers, and their family members being injured or killed.

After more than thirty years of law practice, several cases have prominent recollections in my mind. In one case, which was the result of distracted driving, a family lost their elderly father due to an automobile collision. One of the children was driving with her father as a passenger on a small city road. The driver of the other vehicle which was traveling in the opposite direction was apparently texting while driving. That driver made a left-hand turn in front of my client's vehicle and, even though my client's daughter did her best to avoid the collision, she was not able to do so, and her elderly father suffered some fairly extensive injuries. He was transported by ambulance to the hospital, he was treated, and he was released. After a few days, his injuries seemed to worsen. He was having problems breathing and he was suffering from some cognitive issues. He was taken back to the hospital for treatment and was eventually moved into a rehabilitation/nursing home. Within a relatively short period of time, the gentleman died as a result of injuries he sustained in the vehicle collision. This is what we call a classic "wrongful death" claim, where the injured person died as a result of the negligent or wrongful acts of another person.

My client was already a widower, so my firm represented his children in making a claim against the other driver's insurance company. A settlement was reached for the full policy limits of liability insurance coverage, to help compensate these adult children for the losses that they sustained: significant medical expenses, funeral and cemetery expenses, and the loss of their loving father. Although we attempted to provide financial compensation for the client's family members for their father's loss and medical bills, the loss of a loved one is the most tragic type of case that we deal with as personal injury attorneys, trying to compensate families for the terrible grief incurred when a death occurs as the result of another's negligence.

Obviously, the worst situation in personal injury cases is when someone is catastrophically injured or killed. Many times, in vehicle collisions causing injuries, these injuries may result in permanent disfigurement or long-term damage and treatment. There obviously must be a level of responsibility when driving vehicles that weigh thousands of pounds so as to avoid their being used as destructive machines, causing damages and injuries. Drivers should have no choice other than to be careful, cautious, and to always keep in mind that their primary task while driving is to drive safely, keeping their eyes on the road in front of them.

PROTECT YOUR FAMILY WITH THE RIGHT INSURANCE

Ultimately, people need to be responsible for themselves and their families. They need to make sure that they have the best financial protection possible in case they are injured due to another person's negligence or fault. It is necessary for people to review, on a regular basis, their own insurance policies: automobile insurance, homeowner's insurance, renter's insurance, personal umbrella policy insurance, health insurance, disability insurance, etc. Sufficient insurance coverage is necessary for people to protect themselves and their loved ones in the event that they are injured and need medical care, miss time from their employment, lose their job as a result of an injury, or die as the result of an accident. I encourage people to carry the maximum amount of insurance coverage that they can reasonably afford, including a personal umbrella policy of insurance. Sufficient liability insurance coverage will provide personal protection in the event that a person causes an accident or injuries to another, as well as provide personal protection in the event that they are involved in an accident in which the person at fault does not have any insurance or sufficient insurance coverage to pay necessary medical bills, property damage, lost income, and pain and suffering for injuries sustained.

Lastly, I sincerely hope that injured individuals are never afraid to consult with an experienced, competent, and caring personal injury attorney. As I mentioned earlier, most reputable personal injury attorneys are willing to provide a free consultation, so that individuals can ask questions and find out their legal rights on important topics such as types of damages for which they can claim recovery, ways to make a claim, and the best ways to obtain compensation for their damages and injuries. A free consultation will help to alleviate the stress that comes with any injury situation, and the injured person should not feel embarrassed by consulting with an attorney. The injured victim is simply gaining knowledge and information and is certainly not doing anything wrong. As explained earlier, in the majority of situations, injury claims are made and settled without any lawsuit needing to be filed and without any personal liability being contemplated against the at-fault party.

As lawyers, it is also important for us to be teachers. We should want to educate the public about their rights under the law and what we can do to help injured individuals receive compensation for their injuries and damages. I will reiterate that I am never inclined to make more out of a claim or obtain more money than a client deserves. However, all clients should have the ability to receive full compensation for their injuries and damages, and hopefully be made "whole," so as to allow them to be put back into the same place as they were prior to the accident, especially when they are not at fault in causing the injuries and damages they sustained. I want to walk victims through the claims process so they know what to expect. However, I also want them to know that they are part of the team involved in helping them to gain justice for the injuries and damages they sustained.

As experienced personal injury attorneys, I and others like me try our best to reduce the stress and daily hassles of clients who have had the misfortune of suffering an accident and injuries, so clients can concentrate on their recovery, receive the necessary medical care they need, return to work as soon as possible, and get back to their activities of daily living. We wish and hope that all of our clients can quickly return to enjoying their lives and avoid having long-term, on-going problems that too often can result from accidents and injuries. By contacting an experienced personal injury attorney for information, people can make informed decisions about whether or not they should retain an attorney. They can also interview attorneys to decide which attorney might be best to represent them in their personal injury case and whether the attorney can assist them to maximize their recovery. Lastly, individuals should feel comfortable that their attorney can assist them to avoid the many pitfalls and traps that unwary individuals can encounter as they deal with insurance companies, while allowing themselves the ability to receive treatment for their injuries, and ultimately get compensated for their damages.

(This content should be used for informational purposes only. It does not create an attorney-client relationship with any reader and should not be construed as legal advice. If you need legal advice, please contact an attorney in your community who can assess the specifics of your situation.)

5

BE PREPARED, FLORIDA HAS ONE OF THE HIGHEST AUTOMOBILE ACCIDENT RATES OF ANY STATE

by Zackary Melkonian, Esq.

Zackary Melkonian, Esq.
Melkonian, P.A.
Tampa, Florida

Zack is dedicated to taking your business personally. He will always "fight the good fight" and is truly an advocate for injury victims everywhere. He is committed to providing his clients with competent and zealous representation, and he understands the hardship his clients experience as a result of an accident and injury. Furthermore, he is dedicated to your well-being and it is his goal to make you whole, both physically and financially.

He received his law degree from Thomas M. Cooley Law School in Michigan. He is a member of the Florida Bar Association, the Association of Trial Lawyers of America, and the Academy of Florida Trial Lawyers.

He started his own law firm in 1998 and has been serving the residents of Florida in personal injury cases ever since.

BE PREPARED, FLORIDA HAS ONE OF THE HIGHEST AUTOMOBILE ACCIDENT RATES OF ANY STATE

Let's face it, nobody wakes up in the morning trembling with trepidation for fear of driving the family car to work and possibly becoming involved in an automobile accident. Unfortunately, you can become involved in an automobile accident in the blink of an eye.

Florida, for example, is one of the world's largest tourist destinations and has one of the highest accident rates of any state. People from all over the world come to visit Florida and they bring with them different driving customs and traditions (rules of the road). Many of them are distracted while they are driving because they are in a new city and are sightseeing while driving. The probability of getting into an automobile accident increases significantly when a driver is distracted, which is why we have an unusually high automobile accident rate in Florida.

Unfortunately, drivers on our roads today don't know the first thing about what to do or what they can expect to happen after being involved and injured in a car crash. It's pretty stressful stuff dealing with the results of an accident you did not ask to be in and hadn't contemplated. You did not do anything wrong. The other driver was the negligent party, yet you're the one that's got to deal with the aftermath. Just remember if this does happen to you, it will happen in a blink of an eye. Chances are you won't even see it coming. What will you do? Where will you go? Whom will you call for help? This is why it makes sense to find a good crash lawyer in your city or town before you need one. When choosing a good crash lawyer, experience, professionalism, and just plain old feeling comfortable with him is very important. Keep him or her on speed dial because you never know when the unexpected will happen.

The problems you will face immediately after a motor vehicle accident will depend on the nature and severity of the accident, which will determine the level of pain and suffering, medical attention, and out-of-pocket expenses a crash victim will have to endure. The more catastrophic the accident doesn't necessary mean the greater likelihood of a heightened degree of pain and suffering. Over the past sixteen years, I have been involved with many cases in which minor fender bender crashes have resulted in serious injury. People need to know that even minor impact-type collisions can cause significant bodily injury, resulting in compensable money damages. An accident victim may have immediate and significant quality-of-life changes as a result of the accident: a lost wage claim, property damage issues, other out-of-pocket expenses.

After being involved in an automobile accident, you may find the insurance companies for both the careless driver and accident victim will call repeatedly to ask questions (some very personal in nature) regarding the accident and the resulting damages sustained. You need to be careful what you say to an insurance adjuster, as your responses may be used against you by the insurance company at trial or during the settlement or negotiation phase of your case.

My best advice, never give an insurance company a statement of any kind, either verbal or in writing, without counsel either being present or having an opportunity to review the document(s) you are asked to sign. In fact, a client should never under any circumstances discuss the details of his or her accident or injuries with persons not entitled to that information. Any inquiries from the person who caused your injuries or his representative should be referred directly to your lawyer. If the careless driver's insurance carrier contacts you without the presence of a lawyer, simply inform the carrier that you have retained counsel and provide them with the lawyer's name, phone number, and address, if available. Your lawyer will represent you regarding any questions about the accident they may have. If you have already made a statement to any insurance company representative or anyone else prior to retaining a lawyer, immediately inform the lawyer, upon retainer of his services, of these statements and the contents of said statements, and provide your law firm with the name and contact information of the person(s) who took your statement. Being forthcoming and honest with your lawyer goes a long way in building the relationship required for a successful result in your claim.

HIRING A PERSONAL INJURY LAWYER IS THE MOST PRUDENT THING YOU CAN DO IF YOU ARE INJURED IN AN ACCIDENT

I find it very baffling when a crash victim comes into my office expressing great concern with the many troubling issues that now face him or her, yet still feeling some apprehension, as to whether or not he or she should hire a lawyer to help him or her through this uncharted territory. The lawyers I know take their profession very seriously. These are honest, hard-working women and men who devote their lives to helping others.

We all purchase automobile insurance to protect our cars in case of property damage due to a collision, so it only stands to reason that people should hire a crash lawyer to protect their bodies from personal injury as a result of those same collisions. People need to care more about themselves and less about their stuff. Hiring a lawyer to protect your interest is not about being greedy or litigious. It's about justice and what's right. It's about being responsible to yourself and your family. It's about your health. And it's about being entitled to what you're going to need to put you in the same position you were in before the accident ever took place and more.

If injured in an automobile accident, hiring a lawyer is the most prudent thing a person can do. In most cases, your crash lawyer can help you find a physician to help you with your injuries and document your injuries or lack thereof. It's always better to be safe and see a physician than be sorry for not seeing one.

Our collective goal is to make sure the client gets the best medical care possible in order to cure or minimize the permanent effects of his or her injuries. The client can best serve his or her case by informing the lawyer and physician of any subjective complaints. Then it will be up to the physician to correlate the client's subjective complaints through objective testing and his own clinical observations. This will help the physician make an educated prognosis and diagnosis for his or her patient's current medical condition as a result of the automobile accident.

It is important for you to go to the doctor as long as the injuries continue to bother you. You should relate all symptoms that you have which have arisen from, or were affected by, the accident to your treating doctor(s). It is important to maintain your therapy and go to all your doctor appointments because you cannot expect a doctor to give effective testimony as to your medical condition at the time of trial if he or she has not examined you for several months prior to trial. The doctor would not be able to state within a reasonable degree of medical probability your current medical condition. Moreover, the insurance carriers adjusting and negotiating the claim will often treat someone with sporadic treatment as evidence of no injury or an early cure.

One of the most significant aspects of any automobile crash case in Florida is the permanency of injury threshold requirement. This is a condition precedent to being able to present a claim in court for monetary damages, where the treating physician must, with a reasonable degree of medical probability, give admissible testimony as to the permanent nature of all injuries sustained and directly caused by the automobile accident. A physical body impairment rating of one percent impairment in the state of Florida is enough to meet the threshold requirement mentioned above.

Furthermore, doctors know from experience that the full extent of an individual's injuries may take months to fully materialize. That's why it is important for the lawyer handling personal injury claims to continually request updates on a client's medical condition and be aware of any changes. Furthermore, recent changes in Florida law require injured crash victims to seek medical attention with 14 days of the date of the accident or lose medical benefits afforded them by their own insurance company.

There are a number of services and tasks personal injury law firms provide for their clients in an effort to get them the most favorable results possible, but it is important to remember nothing is possible without client cooperation and a dedicated, diligent staff committed to excellence.

One reason it just makes sense to hire a lawyer if injured in an automobile accident is that retaining a lawyer for a personal injury matter is like paying for peace of mind, without actually having to pay. Upon signing an employment for services contract with a lawyer or Contingency Fee Agreement, you are entitled to competent, zealous, and expeditious representation.

All your communications with your lawyer are confidential and protected under attorney–client privileged communications. Anything you tell your lawyer about your past conduct remains confidential with only a few exceptions.

There also exists a fiduciary duty (trust and loyalty) owed by the lawyer to his or her clients. This requires the lawyer to place his or her client's interest above all other competing interests, including his or her own.

Remember that, in the relationship with your lawyer, you are the boss. The lawyer works only for you, under your direction, authority, and control. A lawyer will never settle your case without first discussing it with you. That lawyer should be able give you guidance as to the current status of your particular state's laws and whether or not the amount of money being offered by the insurance company on behalf of its defendant driver is reasonable. However, the final decision remains yours: only you can decide whether or not you will accept the offer as fair and reasonable. If you do accept the money for your personal injury claim, in lieu of seeking justice in court, the insurance company will make paying the money contingent on you signing a release, releasing the defendant driver and the insurance company from any future claims regarding that particular date of loss or accident. Never sign any document(s) or release with an insurance company without having your lawyer review it first.

FLORIDA'S LAW HAS BECOME MORE COMPLICATED

Another good reason to retain a lawyer is simply that this particular area of the law can get pretty complicated. Therefore, it makes sense that you would seek the assistance of someone with knowledge and experience that can help you navigate through the many issues you will face.

In automobile crash cases, the theory of No-Fault Law has been codified in several states. In Florida, No-Fault Law permits limited recovery for up to 80% of your medical expenses and 60% of your lost wages capped at $10,000.00, regardless of who caused the accident. This money comes from your own insurance policy, even if you caused the accident. The present No-Fault Law in Florida gives injured people who are not at fault for the crash the right to sue the people who caused their injuries ONLY IF YOU HAVE A PERMANENT INJURY AND LIABILITY IS ESTABLISHED.

No-Fault Law in Florida has gone through many changes over my 16 years of practicing law. Tort reform has made it more and more difficult for an injured person in an automobile accident to get full justice. In the State of Florida, any person who owns an "operable" vehicle is required by the No-Fault law to purchase Personal Injury Protection (PIP) which provides coverage for the limited recovery as described above. Recent changes to the law in Florida take an injured person's PIP benefits away if the injured person does not seek medical attention within the first 14 days after the accident.

Also, the car insurance you purchase may have a deductible amount. (I have seen some of my client's policies with as high as $5,000.00 deductibles.) If you have such a policy, it is possible that you may have no right to recover from anyone unless your medical bills and lost wages exceed the deductible amount or you have a permanent injury. If you have other forms of insurance, your lawyer will consider sending your medical bills to that insurance carrier as well.

If you are involved in an automobile accident, injured and live in a state where No-Fault and PIP are applicable, it will be necessary for your lawyer to do some preliminary investigation concerning how the accident happened, to maintain an ongoing dialogue with your PIP carrier to help process your claim for accident benefits, and to continually monitor the medical aspects of your case with your treating physicians until it can be determined whether your doctor is of the opinion, within a reasonable degree of medical probability, that the injuries you have sustained as a result of the accident are permanent. If the treating physician believes there to be a permanent injury, your lawyer shall proceed on your behalf seeking justice for you.

The faster a crash victim retains a lawyer, the faster that lawyer can start working to protect that victim's interests. The initial investigation done by the lawyer is very important in establishing liability, building a strong foundation upon which to pursue damages for losses incurred. It is not enough to establish liability based on "he said, she said."

During the initial phase of a client's representation, the lawyers and their staff immediately begin investigating the accident. The lawyer will analyze the issue of liability and negligence of the at-fault party. The lawyer will also consider the issue of contributory negligence and its effect on the client's position; preserve witness testimony which, if not taken early on in the case, can get fuzzy or cloudy; preserve any physical evidence, collecting and taking photos of debris, property damage to all vehicles involved, tire tracks; and retain the services, if need be, of a reconstructionist and/or biomechanical engineer to help with crash reconstruction and the possible effects on the human body, given the angles of impact and speeds of the vehicles involved. The attorney will also send letters of representation out to all insurance companies, putting them on notice of the lawyer's representation, requesting coverage information from all those that may be responsible for the client's injuries.

In return, the insurance companies will request copies of the client's special damages such as doctor bills, hospital bills, medical bills, and any lost earnings or income that occurred as a result of the accident.

The lawyer will also, as a professional courtesy, help the client with property damage and rental car needs. The lawyer will take the appropriate steps to prevent the spoliation of any key or relevant evidence, which may prove useful at some later stage in the case. The lawyer will, at the initial phase of the case, represent the client during all sworn statements given by the client, including a recorded statement request from his or her own insurance carrier. The lawyer will also send letters of representation out to all medical providers requesting client's medical records in order for the lawyer to keep up-to-date with the client's medical conditions and the possible effect(s) on the case.

Please remember that the aforementioned services are only the initial services provided by the lawyer and do not include preparing a case for settlement and negotiation or, in the alternative, filing a lawsuit on behalf of the client with the intent of trying the case, if so required.

Finally, hiring a lawyer if injured in an automobile accident is, in my opinion, a must. The employment contract or contingency fee agreement you sign with your lawyer clearly explains that, if the lawyer you hire is unsuccessful for you, you pay nothing. You pay no fees for the work done by the firm and all its employees plus the lawyer shall waive all his expenses or costs incurred on the client's behalf for the purpose of representation. That's right, you pay no money up-front and if the lawyer is unable to obtain a recovery for you on your case, YOU PAY NOTHING!!!!

WHAT YOU SHOULD DO OR NOT DO

In order for a client to help his or her lawyer achieve the most successful result possible, the client is in the best position to provide the lawyer with pertinent information, such as the names and contact information of family, friends, fellow co-workers, and people who knew the injured person both before and after the accident and would be in a good position to testify as to changes in the client's quality of life as a result of the accident and overall demeanor.

Also, the client's past medical history and how it correlates with his current subjective complaints caused by the accident is an additional factor that has to be considered when filing your claim. The exacerbation of a pre-existing condition is also compensable and it is the client's responsibility to inform the lawyer and doctor handling the case of any prior accidents and or injuries which must be considered before a lawyer can accurately evaluate the monetary value of the client's claim. Honesty is your best policy. You never want the insurance company to have pertinent information, which may affect the value of your claim, and not provide the same information to your lawyer to even out the playing field.

Other things a client can do to help his case are to keep a daily diary of quality-of-life changes, with an emphasis on restriction of activities caused by the injuries, specific pains and the frequency of them, frequency of medications taken, and the kind of medications. Such a diary will be very useful to the client in preparing for trial should the case end up going in that direction by refreshing his recollection of what he has been through as a result of the accident. Before the crash, the client may have enjoyed gardening, travelling, shopping, dancing, playing sports, cooking, cleaning, playing with the kids, taking walks. All these changes are compensable if they have been directly affected by the crash.

I particularly caution my clients regarding social media and the effect it can have on how you are perceived. Make sure that the image you present to the world is one you can live with. Often, insurance adjusters and other lawyers in opposition will use what they find in social media about the injured person against him. If they find anything which may sully your character or credibility, don't be surprised if it is used against you.

Also you will need to provide your lawyer itemized receipts of hospital bills, doctor bills, ambulance bills, and prescription bills. Keep a list of all out-of-pocket expenses incurred as a result of the accident including travel back and forth from doctor visits and hospital visits, additional help around the house and/or business, including babysitters, housekeeper, pool service, yard service, taxi service. Also include over-the-counter medication for pain or anti-inflammatories, bandages, hot/cold packs, braces, canes, wheelchairs, etc. I recommend that every client keep all empty bottles of medications and all other devices and packaging for the health care products used in his or her recovery. This can make a big impact statement without saying a word.

WHEN YOU HAVE FINISHED TREATMENT FOR YOUR INJURIES

After several months of treatment with a physician(s) and it is determined that the client has reached maximum medical improvement, a lawyer will request and obtain from the treating physician a Final Narrative and all other supporting documentation addressing, among other things, the client's current and future medical condition, the cost of future medical treatment, and any future recommendations. These reports and records are very important to the lawyer as they will be used to show evidence or proof of all the client's losses.

Then the lawyer will prepare and submit to the appropriate insurance carrier(s) an Offer of Settlement for a certain sum in an effort to amicably negotiate and settle the client's claim in a timely and expeditious manner without the burden and expense associated with litigation.

Generally, the large majority of claims is settled without the necessity for litigation. If, however, the insurance carrier is unwilling to make what our evidence shows to be a fair and equitable settlement offer for our client's losses, then the client has the option of filing a lawsuit. If this should become necessary, the lawyer must consider the one or more Statute(s) of Limitations, which may be applicable. In the State of Florida the Statute of Limitation for Negligence-based causes of action is four years. The issue of Statutes of Limitations is very important to a lawyer because failing to file a claim in a timely fashion—four years in Florida—may forever bar, with prejudice, the crash victim from ever receiving justice or having their day in court.

AN OVERVIEW OF THE LITIGATION PROCESS

A brief overview of the litigation process may be beneficial and so follows: Generally speaking, the lawyer will draft and file the complaint and all supporting documentation in a court of competent jurisdiction on behalf of the client, stating a cause of action and a demand for relief (monetary damages) for injuries and other reasonable and foreseeable losses incurred as a result of the careless or negligence operation of a motor vehicle by the Defendant or careless driver.

The Defendant has twenty days from the date of service of process with the complaint, putting him on notice of this action against him to respond or answer the complaint with a formal pleading.

Usually, after receiving service of process, the defendant contacts his insurance carrier, who in turn retains legal counsel on behalf of the Defendant to represent their interests. Generally, the Defendant will then answer the complaint and deny responsibility, deny that the client (now plaintiff) has any injuries, and will often allege that, if it is later determined that the Plaintiff has suffered injury as a result of the accident, the Plaintiff caused or contributed to his or her own injuries.

After the initial pleadings, the next phase of litigation is called discovery, both sides are given the opportunity through certain procedural rules promulgated by statute to investigate the other party and the facts being alleged by them. Lawyers have several discovery methods they can employ in order to obtain information which they reasonably believe will lead to relevant admissible evidence.

Discovery forms include interrogatories (a series of written questions which the parties must respond to in writing under oath) and depositions, which can take several forms but, generally, are face-to-face question and answer periods, taken under oath, in the presence of a court reporter while administered by opposing counsel. Parties on each side will be represented by counsel who is there to protect each client's interests. A good lawyer will work with his or her clients to make sure they are fully prepared and comfortable with the process.

Prior to a jury trial at the courthouse, most judges require mandatory mediation, giving both sides in the lawsuit an opportunity to have a confidential meeting with their opposition and their lawyers. This process is administrated by a Supreme Court Certified Mediator, who shall remain neutral to the parties' positions and is merely there to help the parties facilitate a settlement. The mediator shall have no power, as would a judge, to make the parties do anything. However, should an agreement be reached, the Mediator will memorialize the settlement with or without condition and file with the court the settlement agreement signed by all parties present and their counsel. If, on the other hand, the parties are at an impasse, they will be free to pursue their day in court.

On many occasions I have had clients ask me, "What's my case worth?" There are certain items of damages to which a plaintiff in a civil law suit may be entitled if successful at trial. General Damages, such as past and future pain and suffering and/or emotional or psychological trauma caused by a catastrophic accident are very difficult to quantify, and to make a guess would be nothing more than speculation. Thus, I can only say thank God for our judicial system, which allows all the judges and juries across America to be subjective, based on their own thoughts and experiences, to give value in the form of monetary damages to abstract concepts such as pain and suffering or emotional trauma.

A more easily quantifiable form of monetary damages to which a Plaintiff may be entitled is Special Damages: loss of income; future loss of income and diminution of earning capacity; all out-of-pocket expenses, such as doctor bills; and property damage.

Another form of recovery which may be available to the Plaintiff's family is a Loss of Consortium claim or action brought by the lawyer on behalf of the non-injured spouse for the loss of wifely or husbandly services of the injured spouse in all the ways a spouse renders service to his or her mate and family, including housekeeping, lawn mowing, home maintenance, cooking, companionship, and intimacy.

PROTECT YOUR INTEREST WITH THE PROPER INSURANCE

I know that the world is filled with unexpected surprises, some good and some bad. I have lost count over the past 16 years of how many times I have had to tell good, law abiding people that the car and the driver that hit them and caused their catastrophic injuries was uninsured. When that is the case it leaves me with no alternative but to withdraw as counsel.

You see, without a lawyer finding an insurance policy to file a claim against (bodily injury coverage from the Defendant or uninsured motorist coverage from the Plaintiff) or, in a case where the injured party was injured by a wealthy individual who could personally pay for the damage he or she caused, there's no real money for the lawyer to go after. Sure, you could have your day in court and get a judgment for a certain sum after spending years getting the judgment, only to have no way of collecting because the careless driver has no insurance or any other means of paying. A monetary judgment in such a scenario would be worthless and not in the best interest of the client. This is why, during our preliminary investigation, it becomes necessary for the lawyer to know whether you have automobile liability insurance and whether you have purchased uninsured motorist coverage on that policy. In Florida, an injured person is permitted to make a claim for his or her pain and suffering against his own insurance company if he or she had uninsured motorist coverage.

If I could leave you with some very important and free legal advice, for those of you who live in a No-Fault State, uninsured motorist is the most important form of car insurance you can buy because it guarantees a source of recovery for you and your family from the negligence of another driver. Said coverage is inexpensive and worth the peace of mind. And remember, if you are injured in a crash in the state of Florida, do not hesitate to contact a crash lawyer.

(This content should be used for informational purposes only. It does not create an attorney-client relationship with any reader and should not be construed as legal advice. If you need legal advice, please contact an attorney in your community who can assess the specifics of your situation.)

6

A Good Personal Injury Attorney Will Level The Playing Field

by Steven T. Caya, Esq.

Steven T. Caya, Esq.
Nowlan & Mouat
Janesville, Wisconsin

Steve is dedicated to producing results that help clients rebuild their lives and secure their futures in the wake of an injury or accident. His experience, combined with his knowledge of the insurance industry, help clients understand their legal rights and make sound decisions about pursuing settlement or going to trial.

A partner at Nowlan & Mouat LLP, Steve received his law degree from Hamline University School of Law in St. Paul,

150

Minnesota. As a Board Certified Civil Trial Specialist, Steve focuses his practice on personal injury, both plaintiff and defense. He is a member of the State Bar of Wisconsin, State Bar of Minnesota, the American Bar Association, the Rock County Bar Association and the Civil Trial Counsel of Wisconsin.

A board certified civil trial specialist, Steve was named one of the Top 100 Trial Lawyers in Wisconsin by the American Trial Lawyers Association and is one of 80 Wisconsin lawyers invited to membership in the American Board of Trial Advocates. Steve is consistently recognized as a Wisconsin Super Lawyer by Super Lawyers magazine.

A GOOD PERSONAL INJURY ATTORNEY WILL LEVEL THE PLAYING FIELD

When I think of reasons a person should hire a personal injury attorney, the first reason that comes to mind is simply to level the playing field. The insurance company has several significant advantages over individuals involved in accidents who are not represented by an attorney. In terms of money and personnel, insurance companies have vast financial resources that most individuals do not possess, and insurance adjusters are specifically trained regarding the specific laws in the state in which an accident occurs. Insurance companies have attorneys on retainer or in-house attorneys available for case consultations as well as a vast number of experts, including doctors and engineers. Hiring a personal injury attorney to represent you concerning accident-sustained injuries is a step forward in leveling an unfair playing field.

In an initial consultation, the attorney will begin by asking for background information about you and the particular facts of the accident in question. An experienced personal injury attorney understands that the first step is to investigate the specifics of the accident. For example, in an automobile accident case, an attorney would quickly send someone to take photographs of the accident scene because it may change over time. It's important to preserve what the accident scene looked like at the time of the accident as much as possible. The attorney will also want to interview witnesses while memories and details of the accident are fresh in the minds of the witnesses.

Depending on the type of accident, the attorney will then employ someone to photograph the vehicles involved in the accident, including the undercarriage, frame, and other sections of the car. Also, the attorney will obtain copies of the injured party's medical records prior to the accident. Any prior medical conditions or pre-existing problems showing similarities to current injuries may impact any claims made. Information from employers and copies of tax returns are used to establish an accident victim's claim for lost wages.

A personal injury attorney must also coordinate the various types of insurance involved in the claim. The attorney will place the liability insurance carrier or the insurance company for the at-fault individual on notice. He or she will also coordinate with the client's health insurance company. For individuals who have medical payment insurance under their automobile insurance policy, the attorney will coordinate with the automobile insurance carrier to have medical bills paid as soon as they arrive in order to remove some of the day-to-day stress from the client. A good attorney takes care of the investigation and claims process so that the client can focus on recovering from the accident.

Speaking of medical bills and payments, many individuals do not understand the importance of subrogation rights or the impact of such rights on the settlement of their personal injury claim. Subrogation is simply a concept that allows the claimant's health insurance company or automobile insurance company to seek reimbursement for medical bills it has paid due to the injuries sustained in the accident. For example, if the claimant's health insurance provider pays for an emergency room visit and follow up care, the claimant will also be put on notice that the insurance provider has a right to be reimbursed from any third-party settlement proceeds the claimant receives for the accident. Most individuals do not understand that their health insurance company has this right. For those who try to settle a personal injury claim on their own, they do not understand that they must take subrogation into consideration when they settle the claim. Their health insurance provider will demand reimbursement from the settlement proceeds for any accident-related bills that it has paid.

If a client retains a personal injury attorney, the attorney will request a copy of his or her health insurance policy to review the plan's reimbursement rights. In Wisconsin, depending on the type of health insurance plan, the company is not entitled to reimbursement until and unless the insured is made whole or, in other words, the victim is fully and fairly compensated for his or her injury. If the health insurance plan is a "made whole" plan, this gives the attorney more leverage in terms of negotiating reimbursement rights with the health insurer. Many times, the attorney is able to negotiate the subrogation lien down to a much lower amount. In cases involving an

Employment Retirement Income Security Act (ERISA) plan or an employer-funded plan, the company has very strong recovery rights. Therefore, it is very important to have a lawyer review the client's type of health insurance plan to determine the health insurance company's rights of recovery and the strength of those rights under the terms of the health insurance plan. Remember, the insurer is only entitled to re-imbursement of what they actually paid rather than the amount of the actual bill.

LANDMINES THAT CAN COMPROMISE YOUR CLAIM

While working on a personal injury case, attorneys must be aware of the many landmines that could potentially blow up and compromise the claim. For example, the statute of limitations can present problems in personal injury cases. Each state has its own statute of limitations because there is no uniform statute of limitations that applies to all jurisdictions. In Minnesota, the statute of limitations for a personal injury case is six years, while Wisconsin's statute of limitations is three years. In other states, the amount of time could be less. Furthermore, there may be different statutes of limitations for different types of personal injury cases. The statute of limitations could differ between a medical malpractice case and an automobile accident case.

One statute of limitations landmine is the requirement to put certain defendants (or parties) on notice of a potential claim. When dealing with a case that involves negligence by a government employee (i.e., city, state, county, federal, etc.), a law might exist that requires either the claimant or his attorney to provide notice of an intent to file a claim to the governmental entity within a certain period of time following the date of the accident. Otherwise, the claim may be barred even though the statute of limitations has not yet expired. For example, in Wisconsin, if you are involved in an accident with a city employee, you have 120 days from the date of the accident to provide written notice to the city of your intent to bring a claim. If you fail to do so, your claim will be barred even though the three-year statute of limitations has not yet expired.

Another type of notice requirement involves the under-insured carrier. Under-insured motorist coverage is triggered in accidents in which the at-fault party does not have sufficient insurance coverage to fully compensate the victim for damages. In this situation, the victim may have a right to bring a claim under his own automobile insurance policy. However, in most cases, the terms of the policy typically requires the victim to provide notice to the insurance company of the settlement with the at-fault insurance provider, so that the under-insured carrier has the opportunity to preserve its rights of subrogation against the at-fault driver. If the victim fails to provide the required notice, that failure may waive the right to under-insured coverage. Very few people understand that they have an obligation under their under-insured policy to provide this notice.

Another landmine involves accidents with multiple parties that may be liable for the claim. Any victim or claimant must be very careful when signing a release for one party so that he does not waive any right of claim against other parties. Likewise, recorded statements can be a dangerous landmine for the accident victim. Insurance companies often want to take a recorded statement from the accident victim as soon as possible after the accident; especially before the person has had a chance to meet with an attorney. When an individual is injured in an accident, he is not always aware of all of his injuries or may play down the injuries right after the accident. Sometimes individuals may not have had time to think about what has happened to them, or to fully comprehend the consequences of the accident. This is why giving a statement right after the accident can be dangerous.

A liability insurer cannot require a victim to give a recorded statement. I would never recommend that someone give a recorded statement before meeting with an attorney. The attorney should prepare his client prior to the recorded statement and be present for the recorded statement and determine whether a recorded statement would even be beneficial in the client's case. Furthermore, insurance adjusters use misleading terms and questions in order to obtain seemingly innocent statements that can be used against the person later in the case. Individuals should understand that a recorded statement can be used as evidence in court and it could damage their claim. It is very important for individuals to consult with an attorney before providing any statements regarding the accident or their injuries.

Claims involving motor vehicle accidents are the most common type of personal injury claim handled by attorneys. Of course, the causes of automobile or motor vehicle accidents are numerous: drunk driving, falling asleep while driving, texting while driving, and medical emergencies. Most causes fall under what is called "inattentive driving," which is a serious problem in the United States. When attorneys look at an automobile accident, the question of comparative fault can be an issue. In Wisconsin, as in some other states, a comparative fault statute states that for every percentage of fault assigned to the victim, that same percentage will be used to reduce the amount of recovery. For example, if the plaintiff is found to be 25% at fault for the automobile accident and the jury awards a verdict of $100,000, the amount received by the plaintiff is reduced by 25% ($25,000). Therefore, the plaintiff would only receive $75,000 for damages.

One of the things to consider in automobile accidents is determining the person or persons at fault. This is tricky because fault is not always crystal clear, nor is the percentage of fault assigned to each party. Technological advancements have been very helpful to attorneys in accident recreation so that fault can be properly assigned to each party. For example, fault is in question in one of my current motorcycle accident cases. My client was riding his motorcycle when a parked vehicle attempted a U-turn and struck him, causing catastrophic injuries to his lower leg. The insurance company for the at-fault driver is trying to claim that my client is at fault for a significant percentage because the driver actually stopped the vehicle and left plenty of time for my client to take evasive action to avoid the collision. I have hired an accident reconstruction expert who uses a computer program to recreate the accident in three dimensions. At the trial, I can play the video showing the actual street as it appears in real life including buildings, trees, signs, benches, and bus stops. We can recreate the actual accident for the jury to watch. In my opinion, it will show that my client did not have sufficient time to execute any evasive action to avoid the collision. This technology allows me to prove to the jury that the defendant's theory, that my client was significantly at fault, is incorrect. Attorneys do this in many cases where fault is an issue.

LOW-IMPACT ACCIDENTS CAN RESULT IN SERIOUS INJURIES

Another thing that we see in automobile accident cases is what insurance companies refer to as "low-impact" cases. In these types of automobile accidents, one vehicle is struck from behind by another vehicle traveling at a very low rate of speed, typically between five and ten miles per hour. There is very little visible damage to the rear end of the plaintiff's vehicle or to the front of the defendant's vehicle. However, individuals in low-impact accidents suffer significant injuries. In one of my current low-impact cases, the individual sustained a brain injury, a herniated disc in the neck, and a shoulder injury, among other injuries.

Insurance companies have become very aggressive in handling low-impact cases. Insurance companies often rely on the testimony of a bio-mechanical expert who is highly trained and educated in engineering and anatomy. These experts often state that no one could have sustained an injury at such a low rate of speed because of the nature of the accident. In these types of automobile accident cases, it is very important to have an attorney who is trained in methods of disproving what I believe to be "junk science" from bio-mechanical engineers. The attorney must establish that the quoted scientific theory is wrong and that individuals can and do sustain significant injuries, even at low speeds, depending on the other factors of the accident. Low-impact cases can be very difficult to win. Juries can sometimes be easily persuaded by photographs showing very little damage to the vehicles, along with "forensic-type experts" testifying that this type of accident would not result in serious injury to the drivers. Unfortunately, some accident victims go to in-experienced attorneys who do not feel comfortable handling this type of claim because it is a low-impact case.

Texting while driving is becoming more of a problem in automobile accident cases, especially because this accident-related cause is difficult to prove. While driving, we have probably all seen people texting while driving. However, it can be difficult to prove that the person was indeed texting when the accident occurred. Most people simply deny that they were texting while driving. Proof comes from obtaining the at-fault driver's phone records to establish that the person was texting at the time of the accident. Sometimes, attorneys can even obtain the actual texts that were sent and received. If someone caused an accident while texting, that shows that the driver was being inattentive. However, simply because someone was texting while driving, this does not necessarily mean that the driver will be found to be more negligent than in other cases of inattentive driving.

Proof of texting becomes especially important when the defendant claims that they were not negligent in causing the accident and that the plaintiff actually caused the accident. If an attorney can show that the defendant was inattentive because he was texting at the time of the accident by obtaining phone company records, it can be a very important component of the claim. However, in order to obtain cell phone records, it's typically necessary to file a lawsuit. Once the lawsuit is filed, attorneys request copies of records such as interrogatories and depositions through the discovery process. Attorneys then review the cell phone bills to determine the time that the driver was using the phone to establish that he or she was texting at the time of the accident.

MOTORCYCLE ACCIDENTS

Motorcycle-related accidents are an increasingly frequent and complex type of personal injury case because more motorcyclists are on the road and other drivers are paying less attention while driving. The first thing that an attorney must understand when handling a motorcycle accident case is that some people do not like motorcycles. Some jurors may believe that anyone involved in a motorcycle accident is automatically negligent by simply being on a motorcycle. When addressing these issues, the attorney must be prepared to conquer that type of preconceived bias against the motorcyclist.

Attorneys must also be aware that these motorcycle accident cases typically involve serious injuries. The attorney must also be aware of the legal protections for motorcyclists provided by his state in regard to comparative fault. For example, if the motorcyclist sustained a significant head injury but was not wearing a helmet, it's important to know whether that state's law allows the insurance company to raise that as a defense, or if the lack of a helmet on the motorcyclist cannot be used to reduce damages. In Wisconsin, if you are involved in a motorcycle accident and suffer a head injury, the insurance company cannot argue that your injury would not have been as severe if you had been wearing a helmet and that your settlement should therefore be reduced.

Many times, insurance companies will argue that if the rider had taken evasive action, the accident could have been avoided. It is important for the motorcyclist's attorney to understand the dynamics of riding a motorcycle and whether or not a particular maneuver is even possible, given the circumstances (terrain, speed, etc.). The attorney should also know the riding experience of the client. Did the client take safety courses when

160

he learned how to ride a motorcycle? How often does the client ride his motorcycle, and how many miles per year? What type of motorcycle does he ride? With whom was he riding and was there something about the road that led to the accident? All of these questions must be answered so the attorney can fully understand the circumstances surrounding the accident and prepare a solid claim.

If you are involved in a motorcycle accident, it is best to hire an attorney who rides a motorcycle. He will have insight into how the accident occurred and what it is like to be on a motorcycle. Motorcycle experience is also very helpful when the attorney must address arguments submitted by the insurance company, alleging that the victim is at fault for the accident.

TRUCKING ACCIDENTS REQUIRE YOU TO HIRE AN ATTORNEY QUICKLY

Trucking accidents are another unique type of personal injury case and can't be looked upon in the same way as a typical automobile accident. For example, being rear-ended by an automobile is much different from being rear-ended by an 18-wheel truck, if only due to the enormous number of regulations placed upon truck drivers and trucking companies. What may seem just like another vehicle accident may involve a much greater and more complex problem, especially if there is any suspicion of driver fatigue attributed to the cause of the accident. In that case, you or your attorney will want to check and see if the trucking company has a poor safety record and/or if they encourage their drivers to drive illegally (i.e., driving more hours than they are allowed to drive per day, by law). Secondly, the attorney should check to see if the trucking company or the driver has a history of altering records. The truck driver is required to maintain a driving log that is kept in the truck, and the attorney should subpoena this record as part of the investigation.

Some people do not realize that these trucking companies have a team of professionals that will be at the accident scene within hours, if not within the hour. Their activities will make it difficult for the accident victim to fully recover the type of compensation he or she deserves for his or her injuries. When a person is involved in a trucking accident he or she should, within a few hours, contact an experienced trucking accident attorney because a team will be needed on his or her side doing what's necessary to protect his or her rights. This may include obtaining an engineer to reconstruct the accident as well as sending notice to the trucking company to preserve evidence such as the driver's log, the truck's black box, and GPS data on the truck's location in the last 48 hours. Information like this is vital to prove that the accident was caused by the truck driver, as well as the culture created by a trucking company with an unsafe driving record.

Trucking accident cases can become very difficult if the accident victim delays contacting an attorney. One recent example is a case involving a celebrity who was injured in a New Jersey accident. As reported in the news, a truck driver collided with a limousine, killing the driver and injuring the passengers. It appeared that the truck driver was fatigued and had driven more hours on that particular day than he was legally allowed to drive. This is exactly the type of incident and preservable information that an attorney knows to look for immediately, in order to bring the claim.

In accidents involving trucks coming from Mexico, the first question our attorneys ask is whether or not the trucking company is based in the United States. We want to know the owner of the truck and the driver's residency details. At the same time, while all of this information is necessary, the fact that the truck is delivering a load received in Mexico does not change the nature of the accident or the laws that apply to the vehicle and the accident. If you are involved in an accident with a truck delivering a load originating in Mexico, the accident will still be subject to the same laws and standards as if the load had originated in the United States.

WRONGFUL DEATH CLAIMS

Wrongful death is another area of law that is unique to each state and is governed by specific statutes. A wrongful death claim is basically a claim for the loss of the relationship with a loved one, attached to a certain amount of awarded damages. Wrongful death claims are not claims for lost earnings, although that is definitely a component. In Wisconsin, the wrongful death statute identifies those individuals who have the ability to bring a wrongful death claim, and the maximum amount of recovery for a wrongful death claim. People may be shocked to discover that some states cap the amount that someone can receive in a wrongful death action and that damages can be relative.

If you lose a loved one due to the negligence of another person, depending on your relationship to your loved one, you may or may not be eligible to bring a wrongful death claim. In Wisconsin, spouses can bring wrongful death claims if the spouse is killed in an accident. The cap for a wrongful death claim in Wisconsin is $350,000 for an adult. For example, if my wife was killed in an accident tomorrow, the most that I can recover for her death—a death that removes her presence from my life—is $350,000. In addition to that figure, I could recover her lost future earnings and death-related expenses, such as her funeral and medical expenses. However, the value of her life and the loss of her life to me are capped at $350,000. For a minor, the most that the parents can recover for a wrongful death claim is $500,000.

It may seem odd that you can receive more for injuries if your loved one lives than if she dies, but that is how the law is written. For example, if my wife survived the accident but was paralyzed, I could potentially recover much more money than if she had died. There are certain times when relatives can bring a wrongful death claim. A few years ago, I represented a gentleman who was killed in a motor vehicle accident. He had no children, no spouse, and no dependent relatives. Realistically, there was no claim to be brought under the wrongful death statute as there was no individual identified under the wrongful death statue that was entitled to be compensated for his death.

Individuals should understand that when they lose a loved one, the first thing an attorney should do is to review the wrongful death statute and determine who is entitled to bring a claim. It is typically the wife, minor children, or other relatives who may be dependent on the deceased for support. It is also important for individuals to understand that there may be a cap on the recoverable amount. Frankly, that seems unfair and quite arbitrary, but that is the law.

EACH ACCIDENT VICTIM IS UNIQUE AND EACH CLAIM IS UNIQUE

Insurance issues are another unfair aspect surrounding accidents. After practicing law for 25 years, I have found that it was much easier in the past to resolve claims with insurance companies, who were more willing to pay more money to settle claims, than it is today. Technology is a huge reason for that change. In the past 20 years, insurance companies have begun to rely heavily on consultancy and computer programs with the goal of developing a consistent claims evaluation and payment system. This means that they want to pay the same amount of money for similar claims. Insurance companies are moving away from treating people as individuals in favor of putting accident claims into various categories. If your claim falls within a specific category, the insurance company has pre-determined the amount of money to pay for your claim.

Experienced attorneys know that this is not a realistic approach to take—each accident victim is unique and each claim is unique. Simply because one case involves the same type of injury as another case, it does not necessarily mean it is worth the same amount of money. Insurance companies do not agree with this and would rather categorize claims than treat victims as individuals. Currently, insurance companies are willing to pay a certain amount of money for medical bills, lost wages, and a minimal amount of money for pain and suffering. They are hesitant to pay for long-term care, ongoing medical or chiropractic treatment, or damages for long-term pain and the loss of quality of life. In a case involving serious injury that will require long-term recovery or medical care, you need an attorney. In our experience, the insurance company will not settle the case for a fair value except in a catastrophic situation.

Insurance companies understand that the costs of pursuing personal injury claims are increasing. Since expert witnesses, such as engineers and medical professionals, are needed in many cases, insurance companies have become more aggressive in defending personal injury claims. More and more landmines are placed in the way to block accident victims from receiving the type of compensation that they deserve for their injuries. Insurance companies are aware of the fact that they can probably settle the claim for much less if the victim does not have an attorney. Also, many insurance companies now have in-house counsel, meaning that they hire attorneys as their employees rather than paying legal fees for outside counsel. Even insurance companies that use outside counsel are paying far less for representation when compared to the fees charged by attorneys in other areas of law.

As more and more attorneys have entered the marketplace, insurance companies have benefited because outside attorneys are charging less per hour as competition increases. To earn more money, outside legal counsel need more cases in order to increase the bill presented to the insurance company. This provides a deterrent for a defense attorney to settle a case. Many forces are in place to create issues and make it difficult for accident victims to receive a fair amount of compensation for their injuries without turning to litigation.

NURSING HOME ABUSE AND NEGLECT

There is another misunderstood and very under-reported law-related problem—nursing home abuse and neglect. I believe that there are many individuals placed in nursing homes or assisted living facilities who get maltreated, but no one realizes this abuse is taking place. It is very important for individuals with relatives in nursing homes to be aware of the subtle signs of abuse and neglect. It is easy to see that someone is abused or neglected when there are visible bruises, sores, or ulcers; or the person directly says that abuse is occurring. Many subtle signs of abuse may be overlooked unless you know the signs and are watching for them, such as weight loss, depression, and loss of cognitive function.

Two very important elements in proving an abuse claim are the patient's treatment records and treatment logs at the facility. If you believe that your loved one has suffered nursing home abuse, obtain a copy of the treatment log from the nursing home as soon as possible. Also, obtain a copy of the medical record from the primary care physician to review the orders given to the nursing home, to determine if those orders have been followed. Determine if there have been times when the nursing home failed to contact the primary care physician when there has been a change in the patient's medical condition.

In virtually every state in this country, residents of nursing homes have legal rights. The state statutes can be reviewed online or by establishing contact with an appropriate state agency. People should be aware of those rights when they place a loved one in a nursing home or an assisted living facility. Unfortunately, nursing home care is expensive (especially private nursing home care), and nursing homes search for ways to minimize their costs. One way to cut costs is to hire poorly trained employees or employees who should not be working in a nursing home. Another way nursing homes increase their profits is to under-staff their facilities. By combining under-staffing with employees who have little to no training, these facilities have residents whose medical conditions are far beyond the expertise of the staff. This is the perfect arena in which abuse and neglect may occur.

If you believe that a loved one is being abused in a nursing home, contact the state agency with overall responsibility for the facility. Virtually every state has a department or agency with the responsibility to ensure that nursing homes are operated safely and in compliance with state and federal law. After contacting the proper agency, insist that they conduct an investigation of that particular nursing home to determine if there is an abuse problem or ongoing situation. If you are not satisfied with the response, contact an attorney to conduct an independent investigation. The attorney will obtain copies of your loved one's records to be reviewed by experts. If necessary, the attorney can help you make arrangements to immediately remove your loved one from the nursing home.

The best way to prevent abuse is to routinely check on your loved one by visiting the nursing home. While nursing homes and assisted living facilities often have visiting hours, unannounced and random visits are the best way to ensure that your loved one is not being abused. Stopping by at other times and requesting to see your loved one gives you a better opportunity to see how the facility is operating, or find warning signs: people in beds that are in distress, people who appear to be in dirty diapers, people in beds that need changing, etc. Stop by after hours to see if the facility appears safe, sanitary, and clean and to see if the staff appear to be attending to the needs of the patients. In fact, before placing your loved one in a nursing home, visit the facility several times and take a tour to find out what goes on there on a day-to-day basis.

SOCIAL MEDIA CAN HURT YOUR CASE

A word of caution. While online information and social media can help in reviewing and protecting your legal rights, the opposite is also true. Facebook, Twitter, and the Internet did not exist when I began practicing law. These tools have created a brand-new area of both opportunity and problems in the legal profession. Social media's impact on the personal injury world has been quite profound. Be aware that your posts on social media can significantly impact your personal injury case in a negative way. I advise my clients to avoid social media while their case is pending. Insurance companies, their investigators, and adjusters monitor all the social media websites and will use information from those sites against victims at their trial.

Many people post damaging items on social media, such as pictures of themselves doing things that would suggest that they are not necessarily injured or seriously injured, even when the opposite is true. People post things about their recovery that can be misleading or misinterpreted. In some cases, an individual will post comments about the at-fault party that may damage his or her case. Even jurors have been known to post information on social media during a trial. Some judges now inform jurors to refrain from using social media during the trial. Likewise, social media has created ways for attorneys to communicate with potential clients, which can bring up some ethical concerns. Attorneys should make sure their clients understand the ramifications of their behavior and the effect this may have on their client's claim regarding the use of social media. I advise my clients to stay off social media during their case. At the end of the day, nothing good can possibly come from using social media when you have been injured and are involved in a personal injury case.

For example, one of my clients was involved in a very serious automobile accident and suffered a fractured pelvis and a fractured hip. While he was in the hospital, his mother posted social media updates with comments about how well he was doing and how much better he was feeling. In reality, he was not feeling better or doing well. His mother was trying to make family members and friends feel better about the situation and convince everyone that he was going to be okay and that everything was going to be fine. In reality, that was not an accurate assessment of his condition. It is not just the individual but the family and friends that can sabotage a personal injury claim. In my dealings with social media in any legal case, using social media never produced a positive outcome for the victim, it was always a negative.

I Could No Longer Sit On The Sideline

If someone asked me why I became a personal injury attorney who represents people injured in accidents, I would say that I find it difficult to simply sit on the sidelines and watch people suffer without doing something to help. In the early part of my career when I represented insurance companies, I felt sorry for the individuals on the other side because I knew they were not getting a fair shake. They were not receiving the type of representation that they needed. I felt guilty about that. Thirteen years ago, when I had the opportunity to return to my hometown to practice law, I decided I was going to change. Ever since then, I have represented injured people. Attorneys who represent insurance companies are not bad people. I chose to change the way I worked because I felt like I was able to make a difference to someone's life by being on this side of the fence.

Through representing injured victims, I have established long-term relationships with my clients that I enjoy immensely. It is really nice to see my former clients at a grocery store or just around town several years later. They often tell me how thankful they are that they hired me to represent them and that they tell their friends and family that, if they need an attorney,

I am the person they should see. After 25 years of practice, I still feel really good when the phone rings and someone says, "I want you to represent me in my case." It always makes me feel good to think that there are people out there who think I can help and will give me that opportunity. For many of these people, the decisions and efforts that I make on their behalf impact their lives forever. That is a serious responsibility and I take it seriously.

7

WHY HIRE A PERSONAL INJURY ATTORNEY?

by Isaac L. Thorp, Esq.

Isaac L. Thorp, Esq.
Thorp Law
Raleigh, North Carolina

Isaac Thorp has been recognized as one of America's premier trial attorneys by state and national trial organizations. He has served as a legal commentator on the Oprah Winfrey Show, New York Magazine and WRAL-TV.

Isaac continues a family tradition of fighting for the underdog. His father was widely recognized as one of the country's leading plaintiff attorneys and his great-grandfather was a judge.

174

Isaac is co-author of Thorp's North Carolina Trial Practice Forms in its seventh edition. Thorp's Forms is a staple in law firms throughout North Carolina, and is Thomson-West's best-selling North Carolina legal resource guide.

WHY HIRE A PERSONAL INJURY ATTORNEY?

An injury can turn your life upside down in a matter of seconds. A truck driver falls asleep at the wheel. A defective tire blows out while you're driving on the highway. Suddenly, your life is about hospitals, medical bills, and coping with pain, disability and loss.

If you have been seriously injured due to somebody's carelessness, begin the process of finding a law firm that can help you. The sooner you can turn the legal issues over to an attorney you trust, the sooner you can devote your energy to healing. Find a lawyer who will spend as much time as you need to begin to understand the legal process that lies ahead. Someone who has successfully handled your specific type of case. Finding the right fit may happen quickly, or it may take time. Ask people you trust to help you. But begin the process as soon as you can so that crucial evidence is preserved and your rights are protected.

Why is it so important to have an attorney you trust take action to protect your legal rights? If you don't, it won't be a fair fight. Crucial evidence may be lost. Insurance companies may take advantage of you. You may make a mistake and sign away your rights without knowing it. An experienced attorney can level the playing field so that the legal system works fairly for you.

The right attorney will move aggressively to preserve critical evidence before it disappears. Tire marks get washed away in the rain. Witnesses move; their memories fade. This is especially important when the only survivor is the person who negligently caused the accident. Normally, the investigating police officer will hear two sides to every story. This is not the case when, say, someone is killed by a negligent tractor–trailer driver. Law enforcement officials will only hear the truck driver's version of events. The driver is likely to give an account of how the wreck occurred in a way that protects him. In cases like this, it is especially important to compare the truck driver's account with those from independent eyewitnesses who saw the wreck and to determine whether physical evidence at the scene supports or contradicts the truck driver's story.

An experienced truck wreck attorney will quickly identify eyewitnesses and interview them. Witnesses who stop at the scene and speak with investigating officers may be listed on the police report. Other witnesses may feel it is too dangerous to pull over, so they keep driving and call 911. At Thorp Law, we routinely order all 911 call transcripts and recordings, and interview every witness who might have useful information. Time is of the essence. Some law enforcement agencies destroy 911 call information after thirty days. We also interview law enforcement officials, EMS workers, firemen, and any other first responders to the accident scene. First responders sometimes investigate thirty or more accidents a month. As time passes, it becomes more difficult for them to remember important details about your accident that may not have been recorded in a report.

To build a strong case, you need more than eyewitness testimony. Accidents happen quickly, often at night or when it's raining. Witnesses rarely get the complete picture of how an accident happened.

You need unbiased investigators to thoroughly and efficiently gather physical evidence from the scene and to carefully inspect the vehicles that were involved in the accident. Skid marks need to be photographed and carefully measured before heavy rains cause them to fade. The most crucial piece of evidence is often a tractor–trailer's "black box," an instrument that records precise data about a vehicle's speed and direction and what the driver did in the seconds leading up to impact. This information can be overridden—accidentally or otherwise—if it isn't downloaded and preserved before the truck goes back into service. "Black box" evidence can often establish key facts about what the truck driver was doing in the final seconds before a wreck occurred: how fast he was driving and whether he was accelerating, slowing down, or slamming on the brakes. If this evidence isn't collected and preserved, critical information about how the wreck happened may be permanently lost.

Trucking company investigators often get to the scene an hour or so after a serious accident occurs. It is unrealistic to expect that you will be able to get an investigator there as quickly as they can. Yet acting quickly can make the difference between a weak case and a strong one. Thorp Law has access to a wide network of highly skilled investigators and accident reconstruction experts who can quickly begin a thorough investigation on your behalf. We have a systematic approach to accident investigation which is designed to quickly preserve critical evidence for our clients. Make sure the law firm you select has the ability to initiate a rapid response investigation for you.

Timely and thorough investigations are also important in other types of personal injury claims. Take product liability cases, for example. These claims often involve defective motor vehicles or automotive parts. Recent examples include General Motors' faulty ignition switches and Toyota's sudden-acceleration problems.

If a car or SUV has a defective part that malfunctions, a serious crash can result. If the vehicle is damaged so badly that it cannot be repaired, it will be considered a "total loss." In these situations, an insurance company typically settles the property damage claim for the fair market value of the destroyed vehicle. It then sells the vehicle for scrap metal. Without the vehicle or defective part for use as evidence, it may be difficult—and sometimes impossible—to bring a successful product liability claim.

The early stages of an investigation will include several important steps. Depending on the unique facts of your case, these steps may include the following:

- Immediately taking possession of the vehicle before it is crushed and sold for scrap.

- Putting manufacturers and sellers on written notice that they have a legal obligation to preserve key physical evidence, documents and other information needed for your case.

- Arranging for qualified engineers to thoroughly inspect the vehicle for potentially faulty parts.

- Conducting exhaustive research of government databases and other sources to find out whether similar vehicles or suspect parts are part of an existing product recall.

When you interview attorneys, ask them what specific steps they will take in the first thirty days of your case, if you decide to hire them.

Other types of personal injury cases also need to be quickly and thoroughly investigated. Take power line injury claims, for example. Injuries from power lines may occur when a utility company fails to repair a storm-damaged pole or line that has been knocked to the ground. They can also occur when power lines are installed too close to structures where people may be working or socializing, such as a building roof or balcony. Your attorney should have an electrical engineer inspect the accident site as soon as possible to measure and document the clearance distances between the power lines and the structure. This will allow the law firm to determine whether the utility company violated clearance requirements in electrical safety codes. I'll give you an example.

I once represented a young woman who was severely burned by a power line while standing on the roof of a building. Shortly before she retained our law firm, the utility company that owned the electric lines inspected the scene, took photographs, and measured the distance between the electric lines and the building. The power company then moved the lines farther away from the building. This was the right thing for the company to do because the power lines were dangerously close to the roof.

When we took the case and inspected the scene, we measured the clearance distances, knowing the company had already moved the power lines. However, only the power company knew how close the power lines had been to the building when my client was injured. The company should have freely provided the measurements, photographs, and other evidence that established the distance between the power lines and the building. Instead, it refused to provide this basic information.

The company's attorneys first claimed they did not have the information. Then they claimed the information was "privileged," a legal defense corporations sometimes misuse when they don't want to turn over evidence that shows they were negligent.

I figured if the utility was fighting so hard to keep this information secret, the evidence probably showed the power lines were dangerously close to the building. So I went to court and successfully forced the utility company to provide all of the measurements, photographs, and other evidence about the location of the power lines when the accident occurred. Sure enough, the company's own measurements proved the power lines were located dangerously close to the building and that the company had violated the National Electric Safety Code—the "safety Bible" of the electric power industry.

Delayed investigations help the wrongdoer. If the power company had lost or destroyed this important evidence, my job may not have been impossible, but it would have been much harder.

Trucking and insurance companies, manufacturers, and utility companies have an advantage because they can dispatch their investigators and attorneys to gather evidence at the scene as soon as they learn of an accident. You need a law firm that can move quickly on your behalf.

AN EXPERIENCED ATTORNEY WILL HELP YOU AVOID MISTAKES THAT CAN HURT YOUR CASE

X Insurance companies know the ropes. They investigate thousands of accidents every year. They know how the legal system works. If you don't, you are at a big disadvantage.

Insurance companies sometimes take advantage of people by making a low-ball offer early on, before an accident victim has enough information to evaluate whether the offer is fair. If you're hurting, out of work and the medical bills are mounting, a quick settlement may be tempting. You are in a vulnerable position and need support. You may get a call from insurance adjusters who express their deep regrets for your loss. They may offer to give you some short-term money just to help you get through this difficult time. It is completely natural to think, "These guys are trying to help me. They're on my side." Remember: They are working for the insurance company, not for you. They may be good people, but often their goal is to settle your claim as cheaply as possible.

Your attorney should walk you through every step of the settlement process so you don't feel overwhelmed. With his support and guidance, you can avoid the mistake of accepting a low-ball offer.

When you get a settlement offer, you need to objectively evaluate whether it is fair. To do this, you first need to know *everything* the law allows you to be compensated for. You may be entitled to specific categories of compensation when you've been injured due to someone else's negligence. These categories are also known as "elements of damage." Depending on the specific facts in your case, these categories may include the following:

- Medical expenses
- Loss of income
- Pain and suffering
- Scars or disfigurement
- Loss of use of part of the body
- Permanent injury

Other categories of claims also may apply in your case, and your spouse may have a separate claim for losses he or she experienced when you were injured.

These categories of claims may seem pretty straightforward, but the devil is in the details. If you're thinking about handling your claim without the help of an attorney, please ask yourself this question: Do I know what each of these categories specifically allows me to recover in a settlement? If you don't, you may end up accepting an offer that doesn't provide you with the financial security you need to get back on your feet after a serious injury.

For example, the law says you should be compensated for your injury-related medical expenses. This category includes past *and future* medical expenses. If you're still in the early stages of medical treatment, you may not know what medical care you will need in the future or how much it will cost. Without this information, you can't accurately evaluate the offer and protect your rights. If you accept the insurance company's offer and sign a general release, you may later realize you need more medical care than the settlement can pay for. Unfortunately, you will not be able to reopen your claim to get the money for the treatment you need. An experienced attorney will help you avoid this common mistake.

Another common mistake your attorney can help you avoid relates to compensation for "loss of earnings." For example, if you are unable to earn wages for three months due to a shoulder injury from a car accident, you will be entitled to recover the wages you lost due to that injury.

That part isn't complicated. But a "loss of earnings" claim allows you to recover more than just lost wages. What if you were laid off just before the accident because the construction company you worked for downsized? Since you were unemployed at the time of the accident, you may think you don't have a "loss of earnings" claim.

In fact, you do have a right to be compensated if your injury prevents you from earning as much money as you were capable of earning before the accident. This is known as a "loss of earning capacity." For example, if you can prove that your shoulder was so severely injured that you will not be able to get a job that pays as much as your old one, you will be entitled to additional compensation for loss due to your diminished capacity to earn money.

Again, insurance companies are not required to educate you. If you don't ask, their adjusters probably will not tell you about the difference between a claim for "lost wages" and a claim for "loss of earning capacity." What you don't know *can* hurt you. Don't get me wrong. Not everyone needs an attorney. If you were in a fender bender that caused minor injuries and now you feel fine, you may not need to hire someone to represent you.

If you were seriously injured, though, you owe it to yourself and your family to at least educate yourself. You need to know your rights. I can help you with that. At Thorp Law, we offer free consultations to people with serious personal injury and wrongful death claims. We can meet you at our office, your home, or in the hospital if you're still there.

I will sit down with you and I'll listen to you carefully so that I understand exactly what happened to you and what you're going through. I'll spend as much time as needed to help you understand the legal process and how you can avoid making common mistakes that harm your personal injury claim. I will explain your legal rights to you in plain English, and I will give you my assessment of your case. If you don't need an attorney, I will tell you that. If you do, I will tell you the best plan for proceeding with your case. When your consultation is over, you won't owe me anything.

WHAT ARE SOME OTHER TYPES OF CASES A PERSONAL INJURY ATTORNEY HANDLES?

Some law firms, including many that advertise on television, handle only car wreck cases. Often, an accident involves more than one area of law and requires an attorney who knows how to handle several types of personal injury claims. For example, if a defective auto part was one of the causes of an accident, you will need an attorney who has success-fully handled wreck cases *and* product liability claims. I'll tell you a story to illustrate.

I recently represented a family who lost two family members in a tractor–trailer wreck. This was a tragic accident involving a 22-year-old woman who was driving with her father on

Interstate 40 in North Carolina. Her rear tire blew out, causing the car to veer across several travel lanes. As she struggled to regain control of the car, a tractor–trailer driver, several hundred yards behind, saw her car weaving across the highway.

The truck driver claimed that he slammed on his brakes as soon as he saw that our clients were in trouble. The physical and "black box" evidence told a different story: The truck driver disengaged the cruise control, changed lanes, and kept on driving down the Interstate. Several hundred feet down the highway, the tractor–trailer slammed into the car and killed the young woman and her father.

A law firm that handles minor car wreck claims would not be well-suited to handle this case. It required an attorney with experience handling tractor–trailer wrecks, product liability cases, and wrongful death claims.

We retrieved the family's car from the tow yard before it was sold for scrap. We secured the car in a long-term storage facility to protect it from harsh weather and spare-parts scavengers. Then we removed the rear tire that had gone flat and inspected it. It was a fairly new tire that came with an 80,000-mile warranty. The tire was made by a well-respected company, and it had been driven less than 30,000 miles when it blew out on the highway. The tire did not show any other signs of wear and tear to suggest that it had been neglected or improperly maintained.

Why would a properly maintained, almost-new tire suddenly go flat while traveling on a smooth, dry highway? I hired several forensic tire engineers from across the country to help me answer that question.

Through a series of inspections and tests, we learned that the tire itself had been properly manufactured and was not the cause of the failure. The cause of the tire failure was the tire valve stem. If you've ever inflated your car's tires, you know that the valve stem is the tiny hose on the tire that connects to the air hose. Our investigation showed that the valve stem had cracked while the car was traveling at highway speeds, causing air to rapidly leak out of the tire.

Our investigative team conducted a thorough search of several automotive safety databases, including one maintained by the National Highway Traffic Safety Administration, also known as NHTSA. I also reviewed thousands of documents we obtained from the manufacturer and valve stem retailer.

Sadly, I learned that this wreck could easily have been avoided.

- Ten years before this accident, the tire valve stem manufacturer specifically identified premature cracking as a potential problem that could result in a tire blowout and lead to serious injury or death. The manufacturer specifically identified the remedy as making sure that an anti-cracking chemical compound was used when the valve stems were produced.

- A few years later, the valve stem's American manufacturer outsourced production to China. The Chinese subcontractors produced several thousand valve stems, but failed to use the anti-cracking chemical compounds that had been identified as essential to prevent the valve stem rubber from breaking down prematurely when exposed to heat, air, and cold.

- Nearly a year before the fatal accident, the valve stem retailer had issued a product recall for the defective valve stems, including the stem that malfunctioned on my clients' tire. But the tire retailer never called our clients or sent them a recall letter to warn them of the defective valve stem.

- The tire retailer easily could have warned our clients of the dangerous valve stem. It had sent them ten marketing letters aimed at selling more tires but never warned them about the defective valve stem and the lethal hazard it posed.

After months of investigation and analysis, I concluded that the negligence of the valve stem manufacturer and retailer was clear. They knew the valve stems could malfunction and cause a crash without warning. For the cost of a stamp or a local phone call, they could have given my clients an opportunity to protect themselves. They chose not to warn them, and as a result, two wonderful people were killed.

Now let's talk about the trucking company. Was the tractor–trailer driver faced with a sudden emergency that made the collision inevitable? Or could he have performed evasive maneuvers and avoided the accident?

The truck driver claimed that he slammed on his brakes after he saw my clients' car veer across the travel lanes but wasn't able to stop the truck before impact. We needed to figure out whether he was telling the truth or he was just protecting himself. We compared his account to the observations of other witnesses and studied the physical evidence to determine whether it supported or contradicted the truck driver's story.

Our accident reconstruction expert analyzed the physical evidence and technical specifications he obtained from the tractor–trailer manufacturer about the stopping distance capabilities of the truck involved in the wreck. He was able to show that the driver could have stopped the tractor–trailer almost 200 feet short of where the crash actually occurred through a moderate application of the truck's brakes.

This single, tragic accident involved three different types of personal injury claims: wrongful death, a tractor–trailer wreck, and product liability. After almost two years of aggressive litigation, we settled the case for several million dollars within two days after the trial began.

Let's talk about some other types of cases a personal injury attorney may handle. When you hear mention of a "premises liability claim," you may think of a typical slip and fall— someone trips on an uneven sidewalk or slips on a grape at the grocery store. But premises liability claims can sometimes involve scenarios that are very different from what people may typically consider. I'll tell you about two different types of premises liability cases so you can see what I'm talking about.

My former law partner, David Kirby and I represented a construction worker who was severely injured while building an outdoor movie set. *The Crow*, a movie starring Brandon Lee, was being filmed at a movie studio in Wilmington, North Carolina. The movie studio had leased a portion of the movie lot to the production company that was making the film. Our client suffered third degree electrical burns, a spinal cord injury, and organ damage when the cherry picker he was operating came into contact with nearby uninsulated electric power lines. He lay trapped on the floor of the cherry picker basket, his clothes on fire. One of his co-workers shimmied up the mast to the basket and helped smother the flames.

This case required knowledge of the law related to premises liability, the safe placement of power lines, and landlord–tenant contracts. We also needed a thorough understanding of burn, spinal cord, and internal organ injuries.

The lawsuit was complicated by the movie studio's bankruptcy. The trial itself lasted four weeks, resulting in a multi-million dollar verdict. The verdict was followed by years of appeals to the North Carolina Court of Appeals and Supreme Court. It took nearly ten years, but our client and his family finally got the justice they deserved.

Now let's talk about a very different type of premises liability case: an inadequate security claim involving workplace violence. Kirby and I brought a claim against a multi-national business in a "workplace violence" case in Asheville, North Carolina. Three people were killed by James Davis, a violent ex-employee who went on a shooting spree at his old workplace two days after he was fired.

Davis, nicknamed "Psycho" by his co-workers, had a gun fetish and a history of violence at the plant before he was fired. Top management knew that Davis had choked and threatened to kill a co-worker, had thrown another against a wall, and pulled a knife on a third co-employee. Management also knew that Davis had threatened to come back and "take management with me" if he were ever fired.

Before the managers fired him, they first made an escape plan to protect themselves, in case Davis reacted violently. But they didn't make a plan to protect the workers in the plant in the days after Davis was terminated. Nor did they hire off-duty police officers who routinely provided security for $15 an hour to businesses in the area.

Davis returned two days later, killing three people and wounding another. The case resulted in the largest verdict in the nation in a workplace violence case. The case was featured on *20/20*, CNN, and in the *Washington Post* and the *New York Times*.

Our clients didn't care about publicity. What mattered to them is that their victory honored the memories of their loved ones and sent a message to corporate boardrooms all across North Carolina: Take workplace violence seriously.

A FEW CLOSING THOUGHTS

Many of my heroes were lawyers—Abraham Lincoln, Franklin Roosevelt, and my father, to name a few. They stood up for the little guy—people who were otherwise powerless and vulnerable to corporate and governmental abuse.

Insurance companies earn hundreds of billions of dollars a year. They can afford to pay their lawyers $300 an hour to deny your claims. Power corrupts. Absolute power corrupts completely. When corporations or governments have too much power, regular citizens lose. Unchecked, the Big will squash the little every time.

Most of my clients can't afford to pay me $300 an hour. The good news is that they don't have to mortgage their homes to be able to afford an attorney. I work on a contingency fee basis. I get paid only *after* I get them a recovery. It's only fair.

Without the contingency fee, most people who need justice would have the courthouse door slammed in their faces. The cost of admission would be just too high. Contingency fee attorneys swing those doors open and give you a seat at the table. Access to justice.

A famous preacher once said, "The arc of history is long, but it bends towards justice." That's true only if we fight for it. I am proud to be a part of that battle.

(This content should be used for informational purposes only. It does not create an attorney-client relationship with any reader and should not be construed as legal advice. If you need legal advice, please contact an attorney in your community who can assess the specifics of your situation.)

8

WE ARE THERE TO COUNSEL AND PROTECT OUR CLIENTS AS WE READY THEM FOR THE LEGAL JOURNEY

by Joseph G. Macaluso, Esq.

Joseph G. Macaluso, Esq.
Macaluso & Fafinski, P.C.
Bronx, New York

Joseph is well aware that a financial award will never begin to make up for the pain and suffering that you have endured. However, receiving the remuneration for which you may be eligible can help you to know that justice has been served, and it can enable you to recoup the monetary damages you have lost. He is the attorney you want at your side who has the experience and legal knowledge to aggressively advocate on your behalf to get the results you deserve.

194

Joseph has also served as trial counsel to other personal injury law firms who have trusted in his experience and insight in both personal injury and medical malpractice cases. He has tried cases to verdict in New York State Courts, United States Federal Court, and New York State Court of Claims.

He has practiced in the fields of personal injury and medical malpractice for 24 years. He is a member of the New York State Trial Lawyers Association, a member of the Bronx County Bar Association and has served on the Board of Directors of Bronx Legal Services.

WE ARE THERE TO COUNSEL AND PROTECT OUR CLIENTS AS WE READY THEM FOR THE LEGAL JOURNEY

The nature of my work brings me close to people when some of the worst things have happened to them. Times like when a drunk driver thinks he is sober enough to drive or when the surgeon mistakenly removes a patient's only fallopian tube or when a baby suffers brain damage and dies because a simple test was not performed. It happens all around us on a daily basis. While there are those who disparage the work that we lawyers do, we are there for those who need us at a time when help is needed most. It is invariably a time of confusion, self-pity, and, at times, rage. We are there to help with both the pragmatic questions as well as the bigger and unanswerable questions like, "Why did this happen to me?" We are there, in essence, to counsel and protect our clients as we ready them for the legal journey that they are about to undertake.

The journey is usually a lengthy process with every case in our system moving ultimately to trial. However, relatively few cases filed in our civil justice system are actually decided by a jury. In fact, most cases are settled, dismissed, or discontinued long before a jury is ever empaneled. It is only when a case cannot be resolved, however, that our system of justice charges jurors with the challenging responsibility of resolving the questions of fact presented. Although this may seem simple, it is not. While the court decides questions of law during a trial, jurors must sift through the evidence and collectively decide where the truth lies in the evidence presented. In short, jurors must decide, what really happened between the litigants who are now nervously sitting in the courtroom waiting to be judged. For example, juries must resolve questions like whether the patient was truly in respiratory distress when she presented to her doctor or the repairs last performed on an elevator were adequate or, more simply, which driver disregarded the red traffic light just before the crash. The obligation that jurors assume when they are sworn in to deliberate is profound. The jury's verdict is powerful and can only be disturbed in limited circumstances. It is, therefore, incumbent on the parties to introduce the most powerful, relevant, and convincing evidence available to support their cause. Those who fall short are punished with an adverse verdict.

EVIDENCE IS PERISHABLE SO YOU NEED TO PRESERVE IT AS QUICKLY AS POSSIBLE

As the person bringing the lawsuit, a plaintiff is required to prove the elements of the case. This is done with the use of evidence, whether it be by the testimony of witnesses, physical evidence, or both. Some evidence is more perishable than other evidence. By this, I mean that some evidence is available for only a short period of time, then it is gone. At times, the evidence can disappear within hours of the incident, long before you ever even consult with an attorney.

I learned this concept first hand, many years ago, through personal experience. I once went to an event at a venue with a long and beautiful marble hallway that led from the front doors to the main dining room. Shortly after arriving, I realized that I had forgotten my cell phone in the car and went back to get it. As I started down the hallway towards the car, I slipped on a wet floor and crashed down onto my hip. When I looked up, I noticed that a maintenance person had just come out of a nearby supply closet with a mop and bucket. He was visibly annoyed that I had stepped and skidded through the area of the hallway that he had just mopped. I had no idea that the floor was mopped because there were no signs or other indication of a wet floor. In fact, the dry area of this marble floor was just as shiny as the wet area. As I lay there, embarrassed of course, two concerned people came over to help me up. They asked me if I needed any other help, but I declined. I got up as quickly as I could, thanked them, and went to the car where I sat for a while to regroup. When I walked back in 20 minutes later, the floor was completely dry, the man who was mopping was gone, and the two witnesses who helped me were nowhere to be found.

This is the nature of evidence at times. There is a small window of opportunity to take the names of witnesses or to take a photograph of the condition, and then the opportunity is gone. If this case were presented to a jury, the testimony of the two witnesses, as well as the person mopping the floor, would be important and relevant evidence which would have made the jury's task far easier. In the absence of this evidence, however, jurors are left to struggle and consider certain questions. Did he really fall there? Was the floor really wet? Were there any signs indicating a wet floor in the area? While it is true that witnesses can be located at a later point, the risk of waiting can mean the difference between providing powerful evidence and not being able to do so.

The lesson here is that evidence must be gathered when it is available because waiting may result in losing the opportunity to do so. It's like that old corny scene in an action movie where the hero just makes it under that closing door to safety. Gathering evidence is, at times, a matter of timing. The key is to get through that closing door while there is still space to slide under it.

Some of the most credible evidence comes from that person who just happens to be standing there when it happens. This testimony can be powerful evidence because such witnesses are merely relaying their observations, with no other motivation. Most eyewitnesses will provide their information if they are asked to do so. Their cooperation can prove invaluable. However, it is not always possible for a person who is injured to get the names of witnesses when bad things happen. Naturally, when the injury is severe, the priority is medical attention. Some injured people can be disoriented or unconscious after an accident, and getting the names of witnesses is therefore not always possible.

Even if you are unable to get the names of witnesses at the time of the incident, all is not necessarily lost. Locating witnesses after the event is not impossible. Generally speaking, people are not random. Think about your own habits. If you are like most, you probably walk the same way to work or school every day. There may be some restaurant that you frequent every Thursday night or a church service that you attend every Sunday. The point is that people are creatures of habit. This fact is helpful when trying to locate witnesses. Sometimes going back to the location at the same time or on the same day of the week can prove fruitful. Take, for example, the simple case where I represented a client who tripped and fell on a broken sidewalk and was badly injured. She was helped up by a kind gentleman who was walking his dog, a flat-coated retriever. The incident happened at about 8:30 at night. The client did not get the name of the witness, however, because she was in need of immediate medical attention and was rushed to the hospital. The incident was otherwise unwitnessed.

In this case, the client went back to the scene at the same time, 8:30 p.m., to look for her eyewitness. Within a couple of days, the client was able to locate that flat-coated retriever and the very pleasant man who was walking his dog. This witness corroborated the client's story and was very helpful. In fact, the witness also advised us that the particular sidewalk involved had been broken up for nearly a year; a fact that he knew because he was in the habit of walking his dog over this same route over that same period of time.

Naturally, certain incidents are investigated by police or other authorities who may complete an incident report. These reports do, at times, contain the names of eyewitnesses. Getting the names of witnesses from a police report is easy, but cases are rarely that easy. Also, an incident report will usually only provide the names of witnesses who claim to have seen the event and not those other types of witnesses who might be necessary to prove your case.

At times, your case may require a witness who can testify to details other than the actual event. This is necessary because different types of cases have different legal elements that must be proven in order to establish a viable case. As the person bringing the case, your failure to establish the required elements of your claim will result in the case being dismissed. Take, for example, the simple case of a person who is injured in an apartment building because of a defective staircase. One of the necessary elements that must be proven in this type of case is that the owner knew, or should have known, of the condition that caused your injury and that the landlord had a sufficient opportunity to make the necessary repair. Generally speaking, a landlord is not responsible for a dangerous condition if he did not have the opportunity to know it existed. However, it is not enough for a landlord to defend a case by simply saying, "I had no idea that step was broken." In fact, where other witnesses can testify that the condition was present before the incident, or that the landlord created the condition, a landlord's lack of knowledge is precisely the type of evidence that is consistent with negligence. This is so because the law concerns itself not only with what a landlord did or did not actually see, but also with that which should have been seen by the landlord; i.e., the defective staircase.

The key in a case like this is to obtain the testimony of a witness who can either state that he had informed the landlord of the problem that caused your injury before your incident or that the condition was present for a sufficient period of time before your incident that the landlord should have seen and fixed the problem. In these types of cases, it would seem logical that there would be no difficulty in finding witnesses, because at least some of the residents in the building would necessarily be familiar with the problem that caused the incident.

However, most tenants are reluctant to testify against their landlords for fear of reprisal. In fact, I have handled cases like this where potential witnesses with powerful testimony have flatly told me that they would not testify because they did not want to have "a problem" with their landlord. While we lawyers do have the right to subpoena witnesses and "force" them to testify, I learned very early in my legal career that unwilling witnesses are often struck with a sudden bout of amnesia when the court reporter is just about ready to start typing. The lesson here is that, rather than trying to swim upstream, you must find witnesses who are both knowledgeable about the important details and willing to help. These witness usually exist. Your job is to help find them.

The solution to this problem can be simple. In cases like this, where a person is injured in an apartment building, it is important to consider all of the other people who frequent the building who are not tenants. This must be done soon after the incident or the opportunity may be gone. For example, I was able to locate a witness in one case who was able to provide important evidence concerning the long-standing dangerous condition of a staircase by ordering pizza. Let me explain. I knew that this particular building was near three different pizzerias that all delivered to the building involved. I ordered a pizza pie from each of the three and requested that they be delivered to the front door of the property at issue. I waited for the delivery person to show up; at which time I asked about the building and the condition that caused my client's injury. Not surprisingly, one of the delivery guys was very willing to discuss the defect in question. He told me that he had seen this problem for at least eight months before my client was injured. This testimony was important because it established that the landlord had ample time to see and repair the dangerous condition. In the end, I was able to locate a great witness who was both knowledgeable and willing to cooperate. The only problem that I did have, however, was that I had entirely too much pizza to eat.

Another potential witness that should not be overlooked is often the mail carrier. There is something about a mail carrier as a witness that jurors trust. Perhaps it is the uniform, or maybe it is the fondness we may have for our own mail carrier. Regardless of the reason, this type of witness conducts daily visits to countless properties. This being so, mail carriers are very knowledgeable about at least portions of the residences to which they deliver. This knowledge often includes important information that can be helpful in proving cases involving maintenance issues with property. I have also found that the mail carrier can be a great witness in cases involving the mean dog in the neighborhood that everyone, understandably, fears. These types of cases require that certain pre-conditions in the dog's conduct be met before a dog's owner bears any responsibility for the animal's attack. Mail carriers are both in a position to know of this kind of behavior and are usually motivated to cooperate because of their own fear of delivering mail to the residence with the scary dog.

While tenants generally are reluctant to become involved as witnesses, like every rule in law there are exceptions. Sometimes, tenants create tenant associations where grievances against the landlord are discussed and usually formalized with correspondence to building management. It is important, therefore, to determine in property type cases whether the building has a tenants' association who has addressed the issue that caused the incident about which the claim is being made. I have learned that tenants are far more willing to speak out against their landlord when they are organized. Organizations like a tenant association provide the type of group cover that allows people to feel less uneasy about speaking out against their landlord. Recently, I represented a gentleman who fell down a flight of stairs in a large apartment building. He had to take the staircase down from the ninth floor because the elevators were "broken," as they usually were. When he went down the staircase, he slipped on urine and badly injured his ankle. The issue of urine in staircases is unfortunately, quite common, in certain buildings. This usually occurs when elevators are not working because tenants will, unfortunately, sometimes allow their pets to urinate in the stairwells because it is too difficult to walk a pet down eight flights of stairs. This issue also occurs when drug users sometimes relieve themselves in the staircases with little regard for decency.

When I first met with the client, he told me that the issue of urine and debris in the building was a recurring problem. He also told me that the tenants' association had reported the problem to the building management numerous times in writing before his injury, but no action was ever taken to address their complaints. The client provided me with a copy of a letter, which was signed by no fewer than 20 different tenants in the building, complaining of the putrid conditions in this building; including complaints of urine in the stairwells. This was powerful and compelling evidence, but it was also sad at the same time because the tenant grievances were simply ignored for years. Ultimately, the petition was important in the case as it laid the foundation for the proposition that the very condition that caused our client's injury was an ongoing problem that the landlord had simply chosen to ignore. It also provided the tenants with a sense of justice, as they felt vindicated that their efforts in organizing and complaining resulted in the landlord being held responsible for the conditions about which they had been protesting for years.

While the testimony of witnesses is always important in proving a case, you should know that physical or demonstrative evidence is also particularly important. After all, the old adage provides that *seeing* is believing, not *hearing* is believing. Demonstrative evidence includes things like photographs, videos, pieces of equipment, drawings, and so on. It is the type of evidence that is received through the senses of sight and touch. When jurors sit in a jury box and carefully pass around, for example, the photographs that have been introduced into evidence, they are connecting with your case in a way that they simply cannot with testimony. Demonstrative evidence can provide clarity and eliminate the confusion that may come at times, with oral testimony. Unlike witnesses, pictures do not forget and have no motivation to lie. It has been said that a picture is worth a thousand words, but I believe that this is an understatement.

At one time, getting a simple photograph for litigation purposes was an ordeal. In the past, a photographer would be retained and instructed to speak with and meet the client. The photographer would then make an appointment with the client when they were both available and schedule a visit to the location of the incident. The photographer would then take the pictures and get them developed. A week or two later, I would get a set of photographs mailed to my office. At times, the photographs were good, other times the process would need to be repeated. The process could take weeks, literally. However, this process has been revolutionized with the advent of smart phones and similar devices. Now, everyone is a photographer and videographer. In fact, even while on the phone with a client for an initial intake, it is not uncommon for a client to email or text photographs and video during the conversation. This new method of exchanging information is a great innovation. It provides a quick, accurate, and inexpensive way to gather and preserve important evidence.

The key to this technology is, however, that the video or photograph must be taken immediately. The longer you wait, the more likely the condition will change and the opportunity to gather the evidence will be lost. Take, for example, a recent case where a client's hand was badly mangled by a falling window in her apartment because of a defect in the closing spring mechanism of the window. I was scheduled to meet with the client and her mother the following day at the hospital where the client was scheduled to undergo surgery to her hand. After setting up the meeting, I suggested that the client's mother take a video of the window, demonstrating the manner in which it fell onto her daughter's hand. A request like this would have been far more difficult to satisfy as few as five years ago on such short notice. Instead, within minutes of the conversation, a video file was emailed to my office computer with multiple video clips demonstrating the falling window with a note which simply read, "Is this what you mean?" In fact, obtaining the video so quickly was absolutely imperative in this particular case because, before I was able to meet with this family the following day, the window was repaired and the opportunity for obtaining any video proof of the free falling window was lost.

Some clients have asked whether proving that the condition was fixed the day after the incident is the type of evidence that can be used to establish that the defendant acknowledged that the condition was dangerous and required repair. For example, as in the case above, the question is whether it is proper to present evidence that the superintendent repaired the free falling window immediately after the incident for the purpose of establishing that the window was defective at the time of the incident. Generally, the answer to this question is "No." New York State law does not allow proof of repairs performed after an incident to be presented to the jury, except in very limited and infrequently presenting circumstances. To be sure, a lawyer cannot argue, "Of course the condition was dangerous; you fixed it right after the incident." While the argument does make logical sense, to do so would undermine the public policy designed to encourage people to fix defective things after people get hurt. That is, if you knew that your action of fixing a defective condition could be used against you, chances are you would be reluctant to do so, even though you knew the condition was dangerous. It is a good rule, but the rule makes it all the more important for people to preserve the evidence before repairs are made.

Sometimes the physical evidence that you need to prove your case is in the defendant's possession. Take, for example, the case of a client who was scorched by an exploding stove that was in his leased apartment. Immediately after the incident, the stove was removed from the apartment by the landlord and disappeared. The claim in the case was that there were certain defective repairs made to the stove by the landlord which resulted in the blast. I retained an expert to examine the stove and ferret out the defective repairs but was told that the stove was "missing." Naturally, it is particularly important in a case of this nature to examine the actual stove and determine the cause of the explosion. The client relayed that he told the superintendent not to "lose" the stove, even as he was being wheeled away from the scene on an ambulance stretcher.

Our courts obligate parties not to destroy evidence, especially where it is known that the information is necessary for litigation. There can be very severe consequences to a defendant who knowingly destroys evidence that is important, including summary judgment on the question of responsibility. At times, the need for a defendant to preserve the evidence is obvious, but this is not always the case. Take, for example, the case of a man that I represented who was nearly crushed to death when a huge oak tree fell onto his car as he was driving to work. When I received the call, an immediate investigation was conducted which revealed that the tree that fell onto the client was dead and rotted out. According to an expert that I consulted, the tree should have been cut down long before it fell, especially given that it was directly adjacent to a busy roadway. However, I knew that if we attempted to take photographs and video of the tree's remains, we would have been stopped by local police and told that we were trespassing. I therefore went into court and sought an order allowing an expert arborist to inspect the remains of the tree and to determine the cause of the tree's collapse. The order also permitted us to cut and preserve a portion of the tree. Following discovery in the case, it was determined that the municipality involved did not have a program to inspect the integrity of trees adjacent to roadways, but rather merely addressed the dead trees after they fell.

More than five years later, when the case finally got to trial, the jury heard the testimony of the expert who testified as to his inspection of the remains of the actual tree that injured our client, along with photographs taken by him during his inspection. The expert skillfully explained the cause of the tree's collapse based upon his inspection of the actual tree involved. He provided the jury with photographic proof of both the mammoth size of the actual tree and its hollow inside. This testimony was powerful, convincing, and difficult for the defendant to refute. If these measures had not been taken, however, there would have been no way to establish the elements necessary to prove this case, and the jury could have understandably turned our client away without a recovery.

Another topic which I believe is worthy of mention in the area of preserving proof and evidence is the increasing availability of surveillance video. If a picture is worth a thousand words, then a video is exponentially more valuable. Next time you walk into a store or leave a building or are simply walking down the street, look up. Chances are you are probably on camera. The use of video surveillance, while once reserved only for the most sophisticated businesses and buildings in our neighborhoods, is now commonplace. Most systems no longer use cumbersome video tapes, but rather the information is recorded and stored digitally. The technology has come far in making this type of surveillance easy to use and available for a minimal cost.

If you are ever involved in an incident, you must determine the possibility that the event was captured with video. Doing this is simple. Most video surveillance equipment is fairly obvious. In fact, part of the efficacy of video surveillance requires it to be obvious, because it is often used to deter crime. Timing is critical here. Many video surveillance systems automatically record over earlier sessions. There are a vast number of different video systems, with some preserving images for relatively short periods of time while other systems retaining the images for months or even longer. If you suspect that the event was recorded, let your attorney know, so that measures can be taken to preserve this important evidence.

Video evidence provides the kind of honest, objective, unbiased view of an incident which resonates with jurors. I once represented a woman who was struck down and run over by a car as she crossed the street. As a result of the impact, the client sustained a traumatic brain injury. She was rendered unconscious and suffered from retrograde amnesia following the incident. This client had absolutely no recollection of the incident and could not explain the details leading up to her being struck. In fact, her first memory after the incident was waking up in the hospital a week later. In contrast, the defendant driver claimed to have an absolutely vivid recollection of the incident and was certain that he did not strike and run over our client.

Fortunately, our investigation revealed that the apartment building at this same corner was equipped with video surveillance equipment which was directed towards the inter-section where this incident occurred. The equipment captured the entire event, including the driver's quick turn at the corner and his clear reckless action of running over the client as she crossed the street. It also captured the driver's action of attempting to pull the client out from underneath his car.

Clearly, photographs and video are powerful and can be used to help you if you have a legal claim, but they can also be your undoing. Take for example, one of the newer frontiers in our profession: social media. Our society has become so casual in the photographs and video that we take. The images are taken and posted simultaneously to 500 of our closest friends at a moment's notice. I am not a person who is totally opposed to this type of technology, but the lawyer in me knows that this is not always the best thing to do when you are involved in litigation.

THE ROLE OF SOCIAL MEDIA IN A PERSONAL INJURY CASE

Just as a person bringing a claim can investigate and seek out witnesses to prove his case, so can a defendant. One of the key ways that a defendant will attack your case in court is by pointing out an inconsistency between what it is you may say in court and what you may have done or said in the past. By pointing out an inconsistency, your adversary is making the case that you are a dishonest person and are not worthy of belief. Jurors do not like dishonest people. For example, if you are claiming in court that you can no longer ride a bicycle because of a leg injury and you have recently posted images on social media of your latest mountain biking trip to Utah, you will definitely have some explaining to do.

The question then becomes how much of what you say and do in social media can be introduced into court proceedings and if you have any right to privacy with respect to those posts. Courts throughout the country are grappling with these issues; at times, with differing results. The problem is that people presume that their posts are private, but they are not. Social media has created a highway of information which is personal and yet potentially public. Ultimately, I believe the best advice is to be aware that what you post is not private at all and may be twisted in an attempt to undermine your case.

WHAT DAMAGES ARE YOU ENTITLED TO RECEIVE?

Once you are able to prove your case, the question then becomes what it is to which you are entitled. No matter what the nature of the case—whether it is a malpractice case, car accident case, or product liability case—the plaintiff is in the courtroom to seek monetary damages. Damages are categorized into two basic types: punitive and compensatory. Punitive damages are available in only a small percentage of cases, given that they are intended to punish the defendant for conduct that is grossly negligent, wanton, willful, dishonest, or malicious. In contrast, compensatory damages are designed to compensate the plaintiff for the losses sustained and are available in all injury cases.

Compensatory damages are intended to make the plaintiff "whole," or to return the plaintiff to a position that is as close as possible to his or her pre-accident state. This is an artificial legal concept, as most clients never feel "whole" when they are badly injured, regardless of the amount of their financial recovery. These type of damages, compensatory damages, are awarded in two broad categories. One category covers the actual computable losses sustained and is usually referred to as "special damages," while the other category covers the pain and suffering component of a claim. The special damages, or the "pecuniary losses" as they are otherwise known, include the damages for the cost of medical expenses, lost earnings, or loss of earning capacity, as well as other actual expenses that the plaintiff may have incurred as a result of the incident. These damages often continue into the future and, as a result, a person bringing a claim has a right to seek an award for future pecuniary damages, provided that the claim is supported by the evidence presented.

While it is relatively easy to calculate pecuniary damages to date—as this merely involves locating the correct data and adding up the numbers—projecting costs into the future can prove to be a bit trickier because of the variables involved. Take, for example, a recent case of a patient who sustained an injury to her spinal cord during a routine medical procedure that resulted in her paralysis. Her need for future care will continue long after her case is over. Evidence of her continued need for medical care will certainly be established by her treating physicians, who will testify as to the frequency and cost of the future care. However, this client's needs will go far beyond just medical care and will include the cost of wheelchairs, walkers, bandages, medications, and a plethora of other items which will now be necessary in order for her to live her life. In cases like this, an expert known as a "life care planner" is used to calculate the recurring costs that a patient will need for the future. This type of expert generates a "life care plan"—a plan to care for a person throughout the balance of his or her life—and determines what the costs of that medical and other care will be over time. This type of an expert is necessary to quantify this element of the damages because, once the case has concluded and the jury has gone home, the client does not have the right to go back to court and request additional damages.

Another type of expert upon whom we rely when determining damages is a "vocational rehabilitation expert." A vocational rehabilitation expert is an authority in the areas of vocational rehabilitation, earning capacity, lost earnings, and loss of ability in performing household services. This expert will sift through the available information to make a determination of a worker's level of education, his employability, and how his physical limitations will affect the type of work he is able to perform in the future. With this information, the vocational rehabilitation expert is not only able to prepare an analysis of the type of work that this person can and cannot do, but the expert can also determine the potential reduction in the earning capacity of the injured worker. A vocational rehabilitation expert will also consider the client's background, education, physical condition and determine whether there is some other type of gainful employment that the injured client can still perform and whether there is any potential financial loss that may result from the career change.

The last type of expert that can be used in cases that require an analysis of pecuniary damages is an economist. Upon determining, with the help of the life care planner and the vocational rehabilitation expert, the current and future financial losses sustained, the economic expert will use mathematical calculations to ascertain, among other things, how much money the client needs presently in order to provide for his or her needs over the years that follow.

The second category of compensatory damages are called "non-pecuniary damages," or what most people refer to as damages for "pain and suffering." Included as well in this component of damages is the loss in the quality of life experienced by the injured party due to an inability to engage in activities enjoyed prior to becoming injured. Unlike pecuniary damages that can be relatively easy to calculate, damages for pain and suffering require a different type of analysis. It is a factually-specific analysis which requires great detail from the client about, of course, the pain experienced and the suffering endured, but also the manner in which the injuries sustained have impacted the client's life as a whole. No two cases are ever the same, even where both clients have sustained precisely the same injury. There is always a context to the injury that must be considered and evaluated when presenting the claim. Clearly, the broken leg of a professional dancer has different life consequences than the broken leg of a computer programmer. That is not to say that one injury is more serious or important than the other. Instead, by presenting the context of the injury, the jury is empowered with a more complete understanding of the impact that the injury has had on a client's life.

The other thing to consider when discussing the pain-and-suffering element of a claim is the effect that an injury to one part of the body may have on another part of the body or the person as a whole. Our bodies function by virtue of an amazing coordination of body systems and functions which support and rely on each other for our overall well-being. As a result, it is quite common for damage to one part of the body to create or cause another part of the body to become compromised. Take, for example, the client who injures his right knee and now walks with an altered gait or limp. Over time, as a result of walking differently because of the damage to the right knee, it is not uncommon for issues with the other knee or low back to develop. In addition to this type of secondary or consequential type of problem that some clients experience, there is also a degree of sadness that people feel when they are injured. This is an important facet of a claim that must be explored because people who have been injured and limited can lose out on the things that once provided them with happiness or joy. Sometimes this loss can, unfortunately, be permanent. The key to this part of the damages claim is to speak honestly with your attorney and disclose not just the obvious, but to step back and consider the overall impact that the injury has had on the quality of your life.

Finally, it is my sincere hope that you never need to use any of the advice I have provided. However, if at some point in the future you find yourself skidding on a wet marble floor at a fancy party, just like I did, at least now you will know what to do.

(This content should be used for informational purposes only. It does not create an attorney-client relationship with any reader and should not be construed as legal advice. If you need legal advice, please contact an attorney in your community who can assess the specifics of your situation.)

9

WHY ACCIDENT VICTIMS NEED EXCELLENT LAWYERS

by Peter Ventura, Esq.

Peter Ventura, Esq.
Peter Ventura, Attorney At Law
Worcester, Massachusetts

In Peter, you'll have an advocate who will stand up for your rights in the face of tough opposition from insurance companies. Peter is a former Assistant District Attorney, college/university level law instructor, and a member of the Massachusetts Academy of Trial Attorneys and the Million Dollar Advocates Forum. He has 25 years personal injury case experience, consistently achieving superior results for his clients.

218

Peter concentrates exclusively on personal injury and wrongful death claims and litigation, with a special emphasis on cases that present complex issues in terms of the proof of liability or the severity of the injuries involved.

In any accident case, you can't overstate the importance of counsel who combines fast action with a thorough examination of the details and nuances of your claim to protect your long-range interests. His ability to work effectively with experts such as accident reconstruction engineers as well as medical doctors on the technical aspects of a severe injury case is a distinguishing characteristic of his practice.

WHY ACCIDENT VICTIMS NEED EXCELLENT LAWYERS

In order to understand why accident victims should seriously consider hiring a personal injury attorney to handle a legal claim, it is critical to learn how the insurance industry does business. How do insurance companies treat those individuals who make legal claims seeking financial compensation from the insurance policies they write?

Let's take a look at the culture and business of the insurance industry. Let's also try to distinguish between the public relations campaigns of insurance companies via advertising and the real world practices of insurance companies in handling claims. Simply put, insurance companies are super-aggressive, anti-consumer businesses that worship profit above everything else. Personal injury cases inevitably involve claims for money damages against individuals and/or businesses that, for the most part, have the benefit of insurance coverage to compensate persons who have been injured or harmed. So, the relationship between the person who makes an injury claim and the insurance company who must ultimately pay the claim is highly adversarial. The average person may not realize this. How about all those insurance company T.V. commercials depicting smiling and friendly people who work for insurance companies who are "just trying to help?" The advertising and marketing strategies try to make people feel as if insurance companies are there to help out if there is an accident because they are your friends whom you can trust. However, there is a tremendous difference between the insurance company who advertises for your business and who wants your premiums and the insurance company who later has to pay a claim to someone when an accident occurs. The image of insurance companies on television is one thing while seeing how insurance companies operate in the real world is another. One should also remember that insurance companies may behave one way when trying to administer the lower-value property damage claim involving a little fender-bender accident and another way when they are handling a claim that involves serious injuries and thus the potential for a sizable insurance company payout.

In a case involving a serious injury or substantial damages, the insurance company representing the at-fault party is not a friend or ally of the injured person. In fact, it is the job of the insurance adjuster assigned to handle a claim to deny and defeat or otherwise delay payment of the claim to the furthest extent possible. If the adjuster cannot defeat the claim entirely, it is his or her job to pay as little as possible to settle the claim. The insurance company's profit margin is on the line, in a sense, when any claim is filed. Insurance companies are, for the most part, for-profit institutions; often corporations with a board of directors and shareholders who expect the company not only to make a profit but to maximize profits. Now there is nothing wrong with this *per se*. American capitalism is rooted in the rights of businesses to offer products and services to the public for the purpose of generating private wealth. The insurance industry plays a legitimate role in the American economy. The practical real world problem, though, is not with the motivation of insurance companies to make a profit but with the means and tactics they employ to do so.

To truly understand how and why an insurance company handles a particular claim the way it does, it is necessary to look at the big picture of how insurance companies make money and whether or not the tactics that insurance companies employ interfere with the rights of individuals who are injured and need to file an insurance claim.

Here is a bit of an overview: Insurance companies view every claim made against them as a potential source for declining revenue or profits. If an insurance company can get away with denying an injured party's claim and pay nothing to the injured victim, its profits go up. However, if the insurance company must pay an amount to settle that claim, its profits go down. If a company must pay money on a claim because the claim has strong merit, it will then work on the claim in such a way as to try to reduce the amount to be paid in order to lessen the effect on the company's profit margin. The insurance company will do whatever it takes to prevent a loss of profit.

From the perspective of the injured person, filing a claim is about attempting to become whole as a result of the damages suffered. This is the purpose of the civil justice system. An injured person's claim centers on being compensated for medical costs, lost wages/loss of earning capacity, pain and suffering, and any reduction or diminishment in one's quality of life. Because the insurance company and injured claimants have opposite interests, this cannot be a win-win situation for both. If the injured person is wrongfully denied compensation for damages caused by the negligence of another, the insurance company wins by enhancing their profits in keeping the money that the injured person should have received. However, if the injured person is fully compensated for damages by receiving deserved compensation, the insurance company perceives this as a loss of revenue or profit.

Today's business climate of negotiation and resolving injury claims might very well be the hardest that anyone has ever witnessed. The environment is more adversarial than ever. In fact, it is downright ugly. To understand how all this came about, let's look back and see what happened over many years and how things changed. Historically—indeed many, many decades ago—insurance company profits were fundamentally rooted in acceptable business practices such as good marketing, good underwriting (in terms of knowing who to insure), good corporate management, and good investments in the stock and bond markets. Thus, the methodology of enhancing insurance company profits had been to attract more customers through excellent advertising, being smarter about choosing applicants to insure as compared to competitors, and making wise investment decisions in the financial investment markets, which is where the insurance companies make their real money.

So how did insurance companies behave historically in terms of claims handling? For the most part, they would investigate claims diligently and, if the claim had reasonable merit, they would pay the claim by making an offer of settlement that was acceptable to the injured party. Generally speaking, the insurers did not try to manufacture defenses or excuses or try to grind people down when a claim was made by denying or delaying claims just to see if people could withstand the inherent delays in the litigation system. Basically, the insurance companies, perhaps with some exceptions, simply looked at paying reasonable compensation for claims made against them as a fundamental part of their unique business of insuring against losses.

Well, in the 1950s, insurance companies began to look at new ways to enhance the profit margin beyond the traditional ways of good marketing, underwriting, and investing. The insurance companies came up with some ideas that would forever change the ways insurance companies do business. To enhance profits, they began what was essentially a public relations-propaganda campaign to convince the American public (and thus future potential jurors who would decide legal cases and award damages) that lawsuits were being brought by greedy, unscrupulous people and that lawsuits were bad for society. By demonizing lawsuits they sought to create a prejudice against personal injury plaintiffs who sued for money damages. And, of course, this kind of thinking is still very much with us today, although the propaganda has become more refined and sophisticated and is being more cleverly orchestrated.

Today, we often hear how lawsuits hurt the economy, bankrupt or hurt businesses, and cost jobs. We hear how everyday consumers have to pay higher prices for important products or services such as auto, home, and health insurance premiums. We hear that virtually all consumer products have higher prices because of the cost of defending lawsuits. We hear that physicians are prematurely retiring or moving out of state.

Added to this hype are the contentions that many, if not most, of these lawsuits are frivolous and are devised and master-minded by greedy, unethical lawyers who are trying to milk the "system" for the benefits of their clients and themselves. In short, we hear that the civil justice system, which has worked well for hundreds of years, is now in a "crisis."

Despite its roots in the 1950s, it was not until the 1970s and 1980s that these kinds of propaganda efforts reached a new level and then, unfortunately, began gaining real traction with the American public and especially lawmakers. In the 1970s and 1980s, insurance companies partnered with large corporations in their efforts to demonize injured plaintiffs and, in addition to their propaganda campaigns, began an historic lobbying effort at the state and federal levels which sought to turn the civil justice system on its head. The fundamental strategy was to lobby legislators to pass laws that would eliminate, restrict, or limit the rights of injured persons to financial compensation regardless of the severity or life-altering nature of the injury. These efforts often included measures designed to limit or "cap" the damages that an injured party would receive so that, even if a jury found merit in a plaintiff's case and awarded substantial damages, the jury's award would be trumped and overridden by these statutory limitations, ultimately meaning the responsible corporations (and often their insurers) would not be held liable for the full damages they caused.

The lobbying of legislators throughout the country in enacting "tort reform" laws succeeded as many states passed laws to restrict consumer rights and cap damages as the general public, by and large, was led to believe that the civil justice system was broken and needed to be fixed. By the 1990s, tort reform would reach an even higher level as the big insurers, product manufacturers and other large corporations would, behind the scenes, orchestrate a "movement" appearing to be a grass root campaign in which ordinary citizens themselves would be claiming that there is a crisis in the courts and that the country needs tort reform to stop the lawsuit abuse crisis.

Today, the tort reform propaganda campaigns are still out there in full force and legislators are actively being influenced to pass even more reform legislation restricting the rights of the injured. Although the "public good" is the stated purpose of these reform efforts, they really amount to nothing more than a brutal and inhuman business tactic by large corporations to enhance their profits off the backs of those people who have been become sick or injured as a result of someone else's negligence.

Having looked at this history as background, today, an injured person who files a legal claim can expect to have a very aggressive, anti-consumer insurance company do whatever it takes to deny or delay that person's claim, no matter how meritorious the claim. Whether the tactic is to manufacture defenses or excuses, to call the injured person a liar in terms of how the accident happened, or to contend that the injured party is exaggerating or embellishing his or her injuries, insurance companies are relentless in doing whatever it takes to win and deprive injured people from being helped by the civil justice system. All injured persons who have legal claims must now deal with this hostile environment when they find themselves injured due to the fault of another person or business.

In law firms throughout the country, however, attorneys for injured parties try to educate their clients about this transformation of the insurance industry over time as the real reason the legal claims process is going to take so long and is the real reason a legal claim must be hard-fought in order to succeed. Only with this higher level of understanding the dynamic change in the culture within the insurance industry itself can injured parties appreciate the necessity of retaining highly skilled counsel to help them.

WHY HIRE A PERSONAL INJURY ATTORNEY?

Without the benefit of understanding this new norm of how the insurance industry looks upon personal injury claimants, the average person might not realize why hiring an experienced attorney to handle a personal injury claim is a good thing. Any injured person is at a severe disadvantage if he or she does not retain a personal injury lawyer to handle his or her claim. Only attorneys with a specialized practice have the personal injury case experience necessary to handle the complexities of personal injury law, including the ability to gather the proof required to establish legal liability, causation, and damages and to negotiate with insurance companies for fair compensation. Experienced attorneys who specialize in personal injury law will bring something extra to the process of preserving and protecting an injured person's rights.

Some of the services to be performed for the client's benefit would include:

Examining and documenting the scene of the accident. Obtaining photographs and/or video of the underlying environment in which the accident took place is critical. For example, in an automobile accident case, this entails taking photographs of the accident scene as well as the damage to the respective motor vehicles. In a slip-and-fall case, it would include taking pictures of where the injured party fell, such as stairs or a sidewalk. Often, there is a need take certain measurements as well.

Determining whether there were any witnesses to the accident. All witnesses must be identified, located, and interviewed. Their statements should be taken while the details of the event are fresh in their minds as opposed to sometime later when their memories may have faded. In some circumstances, personal injury attorneys hire private investigators to interview witnesses and assist with the recording of written statements.

Searching public documents for relevant evidence. Sometimes public authorities, such as police departments, investigate accidents and, in the course of doing so, obtain significant relevant evidence. This evidence must be acquired as it may greatly aid the proof of the injured party's claim. Often, such public authorities identify witnesses, take photos and measurements, or collect other relevant information. Some of that information may be obtained by obtaining public records through the Freedom of Information Act or similar state laws.

Filing applicable notices of injury claims. Assuming that the initial factual investigation leads to a preliminary assessment that a valid negligence claim can be presented against a third party (person or business), the lawyer's next task is to issue the required notices to all relevant parties regarding the client's claim. For example, if someone is injured in an automobile accident due to the negligence of a third party, the driver responsible and his insurance company should be put on notice of a legal claim. Other notices may be required as well. For example, in automobile accident cases in

Massachusetts, personal injury protection (PIP) claims need be filed to obtain medical bill reimbursement and/or obtain lost wage reimbursement. Health insurers may need to be put on notice as well.

Documenting medical injuries. Another important task is for the attorney to acquire medical documentation which proves what injuries are causally related to the accident at issue. In this regard, the attorney will typically request all of the client's medical records and bills which relate to the client's treatment after the accident. Damages cannot be speculative; they must be proven by reliable medical opinion.

Determining the injury and obtaining a proper diagnosis is an important element of a personal injury case. Attorneys must intimately understand the nature and seriousness of the injury with which they are dealing. Ultimately, the attorney will need to determine whether the medical condition affecting the client is permanent, what (if any) functional disability results, and how such injury affects the client's ability to work and quality of life. Sometimes treating physicians will agree to provide the necessary medical reports and opinions which the case requires, while in some circumstances, non-treating medical experts will need to be retained by the attorney to assist in the documentation and presentation of the injured party's medical damages.

Documenting the client's employment status and lost wages/loss of earning capacity. As with all other damages, lost earning capacity must be documented and proven and must not be left for speculation. The lawyer will customarily send a form to the client's employer (i.e., a Wage and Salary Verification Form) to confirm whom the client works for, the client's job title, the client's duties and responsibilities, the number of hours he or she works per week, and the rate of pay, including any overtime. Sometimes the lawyer will acquire copies of the client's previous tax returns as part of the documentation of damages for lost wages/loss of earning capacity. The attorney will also need to investigate whether any injury suffered will have long term consequences whereby the future earning capacity of the client has been impaired or diminished, causing economic losses in the future.

Researching applicable law and developing a theory of liability. This may include researching the applicable law that applies to the case which may include federal or state statutes, regulations, and even common law case precedent. For example, in a premise liability/slip-and-fall case, an attorney will investigate whether the subject property complied with or violated state building or sanitary codes. Ultimately, the lawyer develops what is called a "theory of liability" or a proposition of how the defendant's behavior was negligent under law and how that negligence was the proximate cause of the accident and resulting damages. Ultimately, an attorney will need to present this theory of liability to the insurance claims adjuster to support the claim, and if the case cannot be settled, this theory of liability will be articulated before a judge or jury.

Preparing a settlement demand to resolve the claim. Most often, a lawyer makes a "demand to settle" with the responsible party's insurance company. This can be done without a lawsuit being filed in an effort to resolve the claim without formal litigation. Accordingly, the lawyer would write a letter to the insurance company outlining the facts which establish legal liability, the facts which establish the client's damages (along with supporting documentation, such as medical records and bills), and such demand would typically include the presentment of a specific monetary amount to settle the claim. If a settlement is not reached, however, the lawyer needs to be prepared to go to the next step if the insurance company refuses to settle for a fair and just amount—filing a lawsuit.

Filing a lawsuit against the defendants and conducting formal discovery to further develop the case. In filing a lawsuit against a negligent party, the lawyer will ordinarily seek a jury trial to have the issue of liability and damages determined. However, with a lawsuit filed, the attorney will have enhanced abilities to acquire more information and documents with which to prove the client's case. With a lawsuit, attorneys can issue subpoenas compelling individuals and businesses to produce documents and to be deposed under oath to answer questions. Additionally, an injured party's attorney will have the opportunity to depose and question the defendant or its employees under oath as an aid to proving liability.

Hiring expert witnesses. As lawyers prepare for trial, they can also retain expert witnesses who can assist in proving either liability or damages. For instance, in a truck accident case, an attorney might hire an accident reconstruction engineer to help prove what the speed of a tractor–trailer operator was traveling at when an accident occurred on the basis of measuring skid marks left in the road.

Experts can also be used to prove the plaintiff's damages. Medical experts can provide opinions as to whether injured persons have sustained permanent injuries and what, if any, disability results. Future medical care and costs can be assessed as well and projected over time. If injuries are believed to affect someone's ability to work, experts in vocational rehabilitation can be hired to assess if and how a person's ability to work and earn a living have been affected and the types of jobs an injured person is capable of doing. Economists can be retained to measure economic losses in the future, including the costs of future medical care, as well as provide an assessment of a plaintiff's future loss of earning capacity.

Presenting the case before a jury. In the end, if the insurance company does not pay a settlement amount which is acceptable to the injured plaintiff, the case must be presented to a jury to decide both the issue of liability and damages. The attorney must develop a plan to present evidence and must prepare witnesses to testify. Opening statements and plans to conduct direct- and cross-examination of witnesses must be prepared as well as closing arguments. Certain visual and demonstrative evidence, such as medical illustrations and even video evidence, can be developed to help the jury better understand the elements of the case.

HOW LAWYERS PROTECT AND PRESERVE CLIENT RIGHTS

Even in the best of cases, there are potential landmines which can operate to diminish the strength of an injured party's case. For instance, if an injured party is not diligent in hiring an attorney with the requisite experience in handling personal injury cases, this can be a significant problem. Unless an attorney has practiced in this unique area of law, he will not understand the pitfalls which can doom the client's case. Only highly skilled personal injury attorneys know what these problems are and how to deal with them.

Apart from hiring the right kind of attorney, another major pitfall or landmine in injury cases can involve technical or procedural requirements. For example, all negligence claims have "statute of limitations" or time periods allowed by law within which an injured party must file a claim in court or forever lose his or her rights to compensation. Failing to file a claim in court within the prescribed time limit means that the victim will be barred from receiving any type of recovery or financial compensation. Sometimes statutes of limitations are simple but in other circumstances can be quit complex. Depending on the state, other notice and procedural requirements may also need to be complied with. Only by promptly hiring a skilled personal injury lawyer can the client's rights be protected in this regard.

In fact, all of the services or benefits provided by an experienced personal injury attorney as outlined above ensure that the responsible defendant and insurance company will not be able to poke holes in the plaintiff's case. To further elaborate, with respect to the fact that legal claims require documentation of medical damages, it is important that injured parties receive prompt medical care and also medical care that is rendered by an appropriate specialist as needed. Experienced personal injury attorneys realize that, for legal purposes, medical specialist opinions are often required. Accordingly, lawyers can prevent weaknesses in the case from developing by encouraging the client to seek out doctors who are specialists in that area of medicine, such as a neurologist for a concussion or head injury. Medical specialists are a great aid in legal claims because when they give opinions about the client's condition, the cause of the condition, and whether the condition is permanent, their expertise will add to the reliability and credibility of the plaintiff's case.

With respect to the importance of taking timely photos of an accident site, it should be noted that the failure to do so can be very damaging. For example, when someone slips on ice or snow on a sidewalk without sand or salt, if a photo is not taken showing the relevant condition, proof of such condition later can only be by verbal testimony when a photo would have made the claim stronger. Similarly, not obtaining and documenting eyewitness accounts of an accident is another significant landmine which can hurt an injured person's case, which is why personal injury attorneys vigorously make efforts to locate all witnesses and take their written statements while their memories are fresh.

Finally, one of the most important things a personal injury attorney will do is to protect the client from being taken advantage of by the insurance claims adjuster who has been assigned to "investigate" the claim. Typically, when adjusters are first assigned to the case at the beginning, they request that an injured person provide a "recorded statement" in which the claims adjuster or investigator questions the client about the accident and the conversation is recorded. This is a potentially big landmine and in the vast majority of circumstances, good attorneys will not agree to this procedure. To the novice, one might think that answering questions about what happened is no big deal. But insurance adjusters have an agenda which is to defeat the injured party's claim. So they would typically ask not only irrelevant questions, but questions that are unclear or confusing, and even ask leading questions which suggest a certain type of answer. In short, this is not the proper procedure for the injured party to tell his or her story of how he or she was injured because it is an unregulated environment not under the control of the courts.

Where the insurance company adjuster questions an injured party whether in person or on the telephone, the important point is that there are no rules which govern the insurance adjuster's questioning of a witness, unlike the rules of evidence and discovery which apply in a deposition or trial when any person is questioned. When a lawsuit is filed, attorneys for both sides routinely take depositions in which both parties are represented by a lawyer and certain rules must be followed during the deposition as to how the witness can be questioned. Thus, recorded statements with or without attorneys present are more like the Wild West where there are no rules and, in this context, the advantage goes to the claims adjuster to the detriment of the injured party.

AN EXAMPLE OF INSURANCE INDUSTRY ANTI-CONSUMER CLAIMS HANDLING: PREMISE LIABILITY CASES

Circumstances where individuals trip, slip, and fall and are injured are relatively common types of personal injury cases. People fall and are injured in a variety of ways every day, with many diverse fact patterns and in a variety of environments. Individuals can slip and fall due to a physical structural defect to property, typically a walking surface. For example, a fall may occur because a customer at a restaurant fell from stepping in a hole in the restaurant's poorly lit parking lot; or a tenant in an apartment complex may fall because a wooden step, which was rotted and decayed, broke and gave way causing a fall to the ground.

The law is actually fairly clear regarding such cases. The law distinctly imposes duties upon property owners and those who are in control of property to maintain the property in a reasonably safe condition for lawful visitors. Whether someone owns a single-family home, a business, or a commercial property, he or the person(s) in control of the property has a duty to use "reasonable care" to ensure that this property is in a reasonably safe condition for lawful visitors. A second principle, called a "duty to warn," is involved in some slip and fall cases where a property owner or manager has an additional duty to warn the public of dangers or defects that are not likely to be known by visitors but which the owners know or should have known exist.

How do insurance companies handle such cases? Typically, when an individual falls and suffers injury due to some defect in the condition of the property you can expect the defendant property owner and the insurance company insuring the defendant to vigorously fight the claim. Defendants and their insurers will almost universally claim, even without actual evidence, that the injured party was not paying attention at the time of the accident and/or that the injured party could have taken measures to avoid the accident. In virtually every so-called slip and fall case, it will be alleged that there was what is called "comparative negligence" on the part of the plaintiff, meaning that the injured party was negligent and caused the accident. This will be claimed even if the defendant property owner was at fault by not properly maintaining the property and by failing to correct the hazardous condition. The insurers will almost always make such allegations even if it is a meritorious claim with objective photographic evidence of a defective condition and hazard and even if the injured party was paying attention while walking. Such insurers will claim the injured party is at fault even where the defect at issue constitutes hazards that violate public safety laws, such as state building and sanitary codes, which exist to promote health and safety and prevent falls and injuries.

CONCLUSION

An accident victim who does not have an experienced personal injury attorney is at a great disadvantage in dealing with aggressive and well-financed insurance companies who are institutionally oriented on defeating or minimizing the value of an injured party's legal claim.

(This content should be used for informational purposes only. It does not create an attorney-client relationship with any reader and should not be construed as legal advice. If you need legal advice, please contact an attorney in your community who can assess the specifics of your situation.)

10

WHY SHOULD I HIRE A PERSONAL INJURY LAWYER AND WON'T IT COST ME SUBSTANTIAL AMOUNTS OF MONEY?

by Frederick J. Boncher, Esq.

Frederick J. Boncher, Esq.
Schenk Boncher & Rypma
Grand Rapids, Michigan

Fred is a founding partner in the law firm of Schenk, Boncher & Rypma. His primary focus is litigation. In particular, he has extensive experience in personal injury and wrongful death cases. He graduated from the University of Michigan Law School in 1973. He is active in many charitable organizations and currently serves as legal counsel for the Michigan State Jurisdiction of the Knights of Columbus.

He has an uncommon concern for people who have been injured by the negligence, carelessness, and recklessness of others. His compassion when working with people who have been injured in an accident is one reason he has so many satisfied and loyal clients.

He also has an insurance defense background which allows him to make an accurate assessment of the case and anticipate the strategies that insurance companies will use against his clients. As a successful trial lawyer, if the insurance company is not willing to provide a fair settlement, he is prepared to go to trial to get what's just for his clients.

WHY SHOULD I HIRE A PERSONAL INJURY LAWYER AND WON'T IT COST ME SUBSTANTIAL AMOUNTS OF MONEY?

This chapter is primarily directed to lay persons so that they can intelligently understand their personal injury case and ask the correct questions of their legal counsel. Any relationship between an attorney and his client must be based upon trust and confidentiality. The attorney and his client must work as a partnership, a team, to properly present the injured party's case, and to work together to achieve justice under our legal system, a system which, although fraught with imperfections, remains the best ever designed by man.

Most people assume that every time they talk to a lawyer, it will cost them a lot of money. It makes them fearful of contacting a lawyer, much less hiring a lawyer. But, this is simply not the case, especially for personal injury lawyers who generally work on a contingency fee basis. Under a contingency fee arrangement, lawyers are not paid for their legal services until the client receives money from the opposing party or his insurance company. It is called a "contingent fee" because the fee is contingent, or dependent, upon success. Contingent attorney fee charges are based on a percentage of the net settlement amount, which means after deducting all the costs of the case, i.e. any costs that the law firm may have paid on behalf of the client. These costs include, among other things, witness fees, expert witness charges, process server fees, deposition costs, etc.

Some states limit the percentage that an attorney can charge under a contingency fee arrangement in a personal injury case. In the State of Michigan (where most of my cases are filed) contingency fee agreements in personal injury cases limit attorneys' fees to one-third of the net recovery. Other states allow a higher percentage fee. Clients can occasionally negotiate a lower percentage figure in cases where the possible recovery is substantial and the risk of losing is minimal. However, it is always difficult to judge initially how successful a case may be given the hundreds of factors that go into evaluating and subsequently prosecuting a personal injury case.

Most personal injury attorneys (but usually not business lawyers, real estate lawyers, tax lawyers, or others) offer a free consultation of one-half hour or up to an hour. Within this time, an attorney can usually develop an initial assessment of the case and explain to the potential client what he or she can expect to occur both before and after the filing of a lawsuit. I always explain the various procedures involved in a lawsuit, including the pre-trial procedures such as depositions (sworn statements under oath in the presence of a court reporter), interrogatories (written answers provided under oath to written questions), requests to produce (requests to provide certain specific documents), etc.

In a deposition, a client is asked to respond to questions posed by the opposing counsel under oath. Other than perhaps executing a will or buying a house, a personal injury lawsuit may be the only time the average lay person has this much contact with an attorney. Thus, it is important for the personal injury attorney to explain procedures so that the client understands the road ahead. Indeed, rules of ethics require attorneys to adequately communicate with their clients.

A personal injury attorney will also use the initial consultation to assess the case. He or she usually will give to the client an honest opinion of the strength of the case as well as his or her perception of the weaknesses or problems which initially appear as obstacles to be overcome to win the case. I rarely will provide the client with a dollar figure of the value of his or her case at the initial conference. At most, I may offer a range of figures to explain what might be considered a reasonable settlement amount. This is because one cannot assess the client's claim until proper investigation, examination of witnesses, and examination of particular legal concepts involved in the case are properly explored. Of course, even after a thorough investigation, filing of a lawsuit, and retention of experts, analysis of medical, scientific, and factual issues and depositions (providing the attorney with a good under-standing of the true value of the case), what a jury might ultimately award may be something altogether different than what either the attorney or his client had expected. What I tell potential clients generally is, "I do not know what the case is worth until I really look into it more and find out what witnesses may say, what documents may say, and what an analysis of the facts may reveal."

Of course, sometimes it happens that what the client may think a witness may say is entirely different than what that witness actually says under oath. I believe it is reckless for an attorney to provide a value of a case at the initial conference given the lack of knowledge of all the factors that go into assessing a case, especially when those factors have not yet been investigated. Sometimes I will give a very broad range, especially when the client has no concept whatsoever as to what his or her case may be worth. In addition, not only does an attorney want to prevent his client's expectations from being raised to too high a level, but sometimes, as a case develops, the client's medical condition worsens or facts are uncovered that greatly increase the value of the case. Indeed, I often caution clients who are looking for a quick settlement that it is important to wait until we see exactly how significant their injuries may be and whether further consequences of the incident may develop over time.

For example, I once represented a man who fell off a step stool that broke because of defective spot welds. The stool only stood about eight inches high. He hit his shoulder when he fell and was taken to a hospital's emergency room to be examined for injuries. This seemingly minor incident with what initially was thought only to be a minor shoulder injury turned into a major injury as the man developed a pulmonary embolism while in the hospital and almost died. He was hospitalized for several months with what had become a major, almost catastrophic injury. The case was eventually settled for a large sum of money. If the case had been settled too quickly, the client might have received only a few thousand dollars rather than the hundreds of thousands of dollars he did receive.

There are many elements involved in assessing a case that a lay person might not understand. For example, if an individual had surgery and a small sponge was left inside his body when the surgeon closed the incision, the patient may believe that this incident would provide grounds for a substantial award in a medical malpractice case. However, several court decisions have declared that failing to remove a sponge used in surgery is not necessarily negligence. During surgery many things are going on at once; the fact that a tiny blood-soaked sponge was missed and left inside the patient could easily happen. Nurses count sponges both before the surgeon closes the incision and afterward. However, a sponge may have become torn or separated, and it is sometimes difficult to tell if the entire sponge or all of its pieces were present on the sponge count tray at the time of the final count. Several courts have thus made rulings that such a situation does not usually constitute a case of medical malpractice. Sometimes accidents simply do happen and no one is to blame. However, it is up to the personal injury attorney to explore all acts of potential negligence as well as all parties who may be guilty of negligence. Negligence is generally defined as a failure to act as a reasonable person under the same or similar circumstances. "Negligence" is what a jury is asked to evaluate, and determining potential acts of negligence is the beginning point for any investigation into a personal injury case.

Obviously, an attorney does not want to accept a case that has little chance of success, especially when he or she is working on a contingency fee and knows that his or her time and expenses will only be paid if the case is won. Rather than accept such a case, an attorney would rather give one-half to one hour of his or her time without charge to meet with the client and assess the case before committing to representation. Thus, free consultations work well for both the attorney and the potential client, allowing both parties to understand the situation and elements of the case at hand.

Thus, an injured party should not be afraid to consult with an attorney. In fact, I encourage my clients to call me with any questions, even if they believe the question may be trivial. I always tell them what I think they could do about a given situation, and I usually do not charge them for such an initial phone call, even if the question is unrelated to personal injury law. It is important for people to find out their rights in any given circumstance. Likewise, if a person has been sued by another party, it is urgent that he or she act quickly to answer the lawsuit. Otherwise, what is called a "default" may be entered against them and they would have no chance to defend against the lawsuit.

Even when someone is dealing with his or her own insurance company, it is often very important to seek advice from an attorney. Negotiation with an insurance company can be frustrating, especially when an individual cannot understand why either his own insurance company (in certain instances) or the wrongdoer's insurance company will not simply pay the claim. Since personal injury attorneys have experience working with insurance companies every day, it is very important for an injured party to seek legal counsel as soon as possible.

"WHEN SHOULD I CONTACT AN ATTORNEY?"— UNDERSTANDING NEGOTIATION

Most personal injury cases are settled even before a lawsuit needs to be filed. But without an attorney almost everyone (even other attorneys) is at a disadvantage. There is an old adage: "He who represents himself has a fool for a client." The first rule of any negotiation (whether it be buying a house, buying a car, trying to resolve a dispute, or settling a lawsuit) is "negotiate from a position of strength." Whenever people have been injured and are dealing with an insurance company, they need an attorney to give them the leverage to be able to negotiate from a position of strength.

As with any legal question, when a person has been injured, he or she should consult with an attorney right away to see if he or she possibly has a case. This general rule of prompt contact with an attorney applies not only to personal injury cases, but also to contract cases, real estate cases, business issues, and defense of lawsuits. There used to be a Fram oil filter commercial on TV in which the mechanic who was undertaking major engine repairs on a vehicle which had not had regular oil filter changes made the point advising customers to address minor issues before they became major issues by uttering the phrase: "You can pay me now or you can pay me later." The same is true about calling a lawyer when one has a problem. I call this "proper legal maintenance."

Even if an initial telephone conversation from a client who has been injured leads me to believe that the person may not have a case, I will have him come into my office to meet with me. Sometimes I will discover he really does have a cause of action because he was not looking at it from a legal point of view when we discussed relevant facts over the phone. On other occasions,

I find that a person may believe she has a very small case, when in reality she has a very large case. One of my clients once had a case he asked me to try to settle for $10,000. After going to trial, we obtained an award for $3.7 million. The lack of assessment of case value can be a real problem if not handled properly.

Some people may believe they have a case, but are still hesitant to schedule an appointment. I tell people, "Come in and talk to me; the last thing you want is to realize that you wish you had done something about your rights before it was too late." No one wants to discover, five years after he had an injury (after the time for bringing a lawsuit has expired), that what he had thought was a mild or moderate injury became a permanent and debilitating injury. The time for barring a claim for personal injury (known as the "statute of limitations") typically is three years or even fewer. Most people want to believe that they will heal sooner rather than later. Unfortunately, that is not always the case. No one wants to be remorseful about not taking the time to talk with an attorney to assess whether or not he had a case and then later discover that the back pain that will now bother him for the rest of his life no longer can be compensated.

Recognizing most people's fear of contacting attorneys, insurance companies often work to discourage people from consulting with attorneys. Insurance companies are in the business of making money; they are not in the business of paying claims. Even in a no-fault automobile state like Michigan in which an injured party must seek payment of his or her medical expenses from his or her own insurance company, attorneys find that these "no-fault carriers" will sometimes discourage their own insureds from talking to an attorney about their rights under the no-fault laws. Once this person has retained an attorney, the settlement value of a case typically increases significantly because the insurance company must respond to a professional rather than a lay person without the necessary experience. Again, it is important to negotiate from a position of strength.

PRESERVATION OF EVIDENCE

Preservation of evidence is another reason for hiring an attorney as soon as possible after an accident. Since accident scenes are cleaned up rather quickly, attorneys need to obtain photographs of the accident scene as close to the time of the accident as possible. For example, one of my sons was involved in an accident once. While he and the driver who had caused the accident were still at the scene, I was able to show up with my accident reconstructionist and perform an investigation. We were able to clearly determine by the physical evidence on the scene that the other driver was entirely at fault. We resolved the case in my son's favor very quickly mainly because we were able to take photographs of the vehicles while they were still at the scene of the accident. We were able to determine exactly what had happened by looking at skid marks, collision angles, the degree of deformation of the two vehicles, and other physical evidence because we got to the accident scene so quickly.

For all injured parties, it is also important to take photographs right away after the injury before bruising fades or lacerations begin to or totally heal. I suggest to family members that they take photographs of their injured loved one in the hospital as soon as they can, recognizing that the most important consideration is obtaining proper medical care, not winning a lawsuit. Proper medical care should never be interfered with by an attorney interjecting himself into the hospital room.

Just like bruises fade, witness memories fade. It is thus important to talk to witnesses while every detail remains fresh in their minds. A copy of the police report will provide a guideline of the persons involved so that the investigation can be purposefully directed sooner rather than later.

CHOOSING THE PROPER ATTORNEY

Sometimes injured persons seek the distinguished-looking, silver-haired TV attorney (who is often not the individual who will be representing them, and who is sometimes only an actor who promises spectacular results). An injured party should thoroughly investigate or research whoever might be actually representing them. That is not to say that silver-haired attorneys cannot be particular well qualified. (If you look at my photo in this book, you will probably note that I am one of those of the silver hair.) However, what the public should know is that many of the firms or attorneys advertising on TV are simply clearing houses that forward cases to other attorneys in the area where the plaintiff lives. Clients will not necessarily get the "experienced," "trusted" attorney who is depicted on TV to represent them. Just because an attorney advertises frequently does not necessarily mean that he or she is a good or experienced personal injury attorney. While some of the lawyers who advertise on television are very fine lawyers, that person may not be the individual who ultimately represents the client.

Something that the public may not have considered is the fact that insurance companies "keep book" on attorneys. They know what attorneys are willing to take a case to trial, as well as those who simply want to settle their cases with the least amount of work and, consequently, usually with the least amount of recovery for their clients. Your attorney cannot be afraid to try your case if necessary. A few years ago, an attorney that I had known for 25 years confessed to me that he had never tried a case in court. From my view representing the plaintiff in that case, I knew that I could settle the case for a higher amount than if I was facing an attorney who was not afraid to try a case before a jury. My client thus benefitted from that badly-timed confession of the defense attorney resulting in a higher settlement than I might have been able to achieve otherwise.

Although most cases settle prior to trial, sometimes they settle during a trial or even after the jury has departed to begin its deliberations. Your attorney should be able to recognize when to try to settle a case to avoid the risks that are inherent in any trial, but your attorney also has to be willing to try the case to its conclusion if necessary. Above all, clients need to be cooperative with their attorney and to provide the tools and information he or she needs to do his very best to represent you.

HANDLING COMPLEX LITIGATION

Obviously, some cases are rather straightforward and others are more complex. Attorneys involved in personal injury cases should have a network of potential contacts and witnesses— such as biomechanical engineers, accident reconstruction experts, toxicologists, product liability experts, road design experts, trucking experts, doctors and nurses (especially for medical malpractice cases), economists, CPAs, chemists, pharmacologists, marine engineers, or a whole host of experts— who potentially could be called for consultation or testimony depending upon the nature of the case. For example, an accident reconstructionist will be able to use the law of physics, trigonometry, and other mathematical equations to perform at least three valuable evaluations: (1) plot the path of the involved vehicles; (2) calculate speeds; and (3) determine causation based upon expertise. Recently, many vehicles, especially large trucks, have begun to be equipped with "black boxes," just like airliners, which record acceleration and deceleration and even show when a driver begins braking and at what speed.

In one of my cases, a computer printout from a semi-truck's black box showed that the semi was traveling at 64 mph in a 55-mph zone at the point of impact with my client's vehicle. The truck driver claimed that my client pulled out in front of him and caused the accident. Thus, the insurance company offered only nuisance value before trial began. A critical note is that, at the time of the accident (as established through meteorologists and the eyewitness testimony of the responding police officer), the entire area was covered in dense fog, and thus the truck driver not only should *not* have been speeding, but should have been going well *below* the speed limit instead. Through the use of expert witnesses, eyewitnesses, and information from the truck's black box, we were able to negotiate a substantial settlement after the first three days of trial, because it was clear that the truck driver was entirely at fault for the accident.

AS AN INJURED PARTY, WHAT SHOULD I LOOK FOR IN AN ATTORNEY?

As an injured person, you should look for an attorney who has experience, compassion, and commitment. You should choose an attorney who has represented both plaintiffs and defendants, because that experience gives him other insight into procedures usually followed by the opposing side and strategies that are often used in defending (or prosecuting) a case. I also believe that it is helpful that the personal injury attorney has experience in other areas of litigation, such as business or construction law. Due to my business experience, for example, I can sometimes devise creative ways to settle a case that others may not have thought of if their experience is limited only to personal injury cases.

Also, your attorney should be looking ahead to determine how to best structure a settlement. The last thing a client wants is to obtain a large verdict against a defunct corporation or a non-collective individual defendant. An individual with no assets and no insurance can simply file bankruptcy and discharge the judgment debt that may have been for millions of dollars with the effect that the unsuccessful plaintiff who obtained the judgment gets zero. Even corporations often have limited assets or have their asset ownership set up in such a way as to avoid the effects of any large judgment. For example, I know of many manufacturing industries in which the business itself is owned by one corporation, the building in which the business is held is owned by a second corporation, and the equipment used in the business is owned by a third corporation. Often the same stockholders or individuals own all three businesses, but a judgment against the corporation running the business means little if the stockholders can simply bankrupt that corporation and start over the next day with a new corporation utilizing the same building and the same equipment as the first.

Payment of a simple lump sum is not the only way to settle a lawsuit. In some cases, it is necessary to structure a settlement with a company that has insufficient insurance by way of payments over a number of years. Of course, even if the defendant has adequate insurance, the settlement can be "structured" with a variety of ways to pay over time such as periodic lump sum payments or guaranteed monthly payments.

Problems arise, however, when the defendant does not have the insurance necessary to fund a reasonable settlement.

Where there is inadequate coverage, creativity is called for. For example, my business experience has helped me craft settlement agreements (especially as in a case where three separate corporations are really involved in running the business but a judgment can be only obtained against one of them as I indicated above) by obtaining personal guaranties of the owners of the defendant business or related businesses. A personal guarantee by both a husband and a wife can avoid the situation where a judgment is obtained against a husband which debt can be discharged in bankruptcy, yet he may jointly own a multi-million dollar home with his wife. A house which is jointly owned by a husband and wife is not included in a husband's "bankruptcy estate" (the assets which must be divided among his creditors). Thus, the home is not an asset that can be liquidated to satisfy creditors which would include the plaintiff with a personal injury judgment against the husband. For example, I once settled a case for several million dollars, agreeing to take payments from the defendant corporation over time, but securing those payments by taking a security interest (what lay people would refer to as a "mortgage") in all of the stock of the company. Thus, if the company had failed to make the quarterly payments to satisfy the judgment that I obtained for my client, on 15 days' notice we could have ended up owning the company (and this was a company that was really quite profitable—I am a little sorry the company never defaulted on its quarterly payments).

WHAT ARE SOME OF THE POTENTIAL LANDMINES IN A PERSONAL INJURY CASE?

An experienced attorney may be able to avoid potential landmines that can blow up in a personal injury case, provided his client comes to him early in the case. For example, under a standard automobile or homeowner's insurance policy, the insurance company has a right to take a sworn statement from its own insured person. The insurance company will usually send an attorney to discuss the facts of the case and take a sworn statement from the injured person. It is never a good idea for the individual to provide a sworn statement without first consulting an attorney. Just the other day, a mother and a son called my office saying that they were scheduled to give a sworn statement the very next day and that an attorney would be asking them questions. They could not afford to hire me for representation; however, I gave them free advice by telephone such as not to exaggerate, not to estimate or guesstimate, not to be afraid to simply say "I don't know" if you really don't know the answer or are unsure about something. I also told both the mother and son to make sure that they talk to each other prior to their recorded statements so that important facts would not be left out or misinterpreted. They thanked me for my hour of free advice and the only thing I heard afterwards was that it seemed to go well, and that the insurance company did pay their claim.

In some instances, I have resolved issues with an insurance company at the time of taking a pre-lawsuit sworn statement. For example, one time an insurance company was refusing to pay a claim for fire damage to a house based upon suspected arson by my client. My client had told his own insurance company he could not have set the fire because he was buying plumbing supplies 60 miles away from his home at the time of the fire. He even provided the insurance company with the receipt for the plumbing supplies. The receipt included a CPU code which could be used to determine the time of purchase. The insurance company first tried to prove that my client did not purchase those supplies at that time, but that someone else purchased the supplies. Since they could not find any evidence to support their accusations, they simply refused to pay the claim. Fortunately, I happened to have represented the large company that sold the plumbing supplies. I called one of the company's in-house attorneys in Wisconsin and asked for a favor. He provided me all the information from the local store, proving that my client had indeed been 60 miles away at the time the fire was started. We were able to settle the case and the insurance company paid for his losses without further litigation.

Similarly, in a case where my client was only slightly injured but his 36-foot boat was completely burned to the waterline, the insurance company implied that he was guilty of arson. When the insurance company attorney took my client's statement, (a procedure for which I had thoroughly prepared my client) they found that not only was he not in a rocky financial position that would provide a motive for burning his own boat for insurance purposes, but that, as opposing evidence, he in fact owned six very successful companies, had substantial assets, owned a large house on a lake, and had recently bought his wife a $25,000 ring as a birthday present. The insurance company realized that their claims of motive certainly were lacking and consequently paid the claim without the need of any litigation.

The biggest landmine in personal injury cases occurs when a client does not tell his attorney the whole story, either due to embarrassment or a guilty feeling about being partially at fault. In fact, even in court I often repeat what a judge once told an opposing witness, "Telling only half the truth is not telling the whole truth. It is lying." However, if the attorney is told the whole truth (the good, the bad, and the ugly), the attorney can concentrate on the strengths of the case and try to minimize the weaknesses. The attorney can then be prepared when, for example, the other side suddenly drops a bomb that his client stated "x, y, and z" at the accident scene. A prepared attorney can usually minimize the damage by preparing the client and having him ready for questions at a deposition or at trial. In truth, people often say things that can be interpreted in more than one manner and the experienced attorney can prepare a client to explain what was truly meant by any statements which may otherwise appear to be very damaging to a case.

If a client holds something back from his attorney and neither of them is adequately prepared, this lack of preparedness can explode like a bombshell in a deposition or a trial. Sometimes, damage from statements seemingly disastrous when taken at face value can simply be minimized or completely avoided given the proper understanding and preparation. Clients need to understand that anything they tell their attorney is protected by the "attorney–client privilege," which means that the attorney cannot tell anyone what has been told to him by a client without the client's prior consent. In many cases, once a client tells the attorney the truth, what seemed to be damaging to the client is not actually all that damaging to the case. Not surprisingly, clients often do not understand the way facts and statements are used in court. They do not understand that some statements may be totally inadmissible in court, given the circumstances as to who said what, when, where, or why. Regrettably, many clients end up severely jeopardizing their chances of success in their case simply because they are afraid to tell their attorney "the truth and the whole truth" from the very beginning.

Another pitfall encountered in the presentation of success in a personal injury case is the failure of a plaintiff to keep a proper history or preserve evidence. The need for rapid investigation, the taking of photographs, and the gathering of evidence is discussed above. Equally important is the testimonial evidence of witnesses and especially the testimony of an injured party. I advise every client to keep a diary containing a detailed record of all doctor visits, including the doctor's statements and any information given to the client during the appointment. The stated log should also include every detail of daily living the client experiences; such as the inability to take a shower without assistance, the inability to go outside to get the mail, the difficulty of walking across the kitchen and bending over to get a pan to cook eggs, the need to elevate the feet hours every day, enduring back pain for several hours during the day, the amount of pain experienced and how on a daily basis, and so on.

These detailed records should also include notations of what the injured party misses as a result of the accident. For example, notations should be made that the injured party could not attend her granddaughter's birthday party because she was in too much pain to get out of bed. This is the kind of anecdotal evidence that is important to place before an insurance adjuster, a defense attorney, or, ultimately, a jury. Detailed records of the emotional aspect of an injury—such as the daily pain and suffering the injured party experiences, including the aggravation and mortification of medical treatments or the humiliation of recovering from injuries or disfigurement—helps the attorney understand what the client is experiencing on a daily basis. Such a detailed diary also gives the attorney a useful basis for helping the client present organized, convincing testimony at a deposition or at a trial.

The explosion of social media has become a huge landmine for personal injury attorneys. Clients often post items on their Facebook, Instagram, Twitter, or other venues right after an accident showing them hiking, working in the yard, or out drinking with friends. All of these supposedly "harmless" things shared with friends are available for the world to see. Such entries may indicate that the plaintiff is doing well or is more or less completely healed. Photos of the injured party out partying endanger a case, especially with juries. Any smart defense lawyer will check the opposite side's social media accounts and use that information to his or her advantage. As an injured person, one should be very careful about what one does, what one says, and what one posts to social media. Additionally, insurance companies have private investigators who will try to catch someone acting inconsistently with stated injuries. For example, if a private investigator videotapes a plaintiff pulling weeds out of his garden for five minutes, this evidence will tend to negate any testimony the plaintiff may offer under oath stating that he has not been able to work in his garden since the accident. On the other hand, a prepared and honest client can testify in this way: "Yes, I go out to work in my garden because I want to do everything I can do to get back to normal. I can only work for five minutes at a time before I must go in and rest for two hours. Yes, that is me on the videotape, but the video did not show me going inside and sitting for two hours with a heating pad on my back because I overdid a little weed pulling."

Views on social media bring up another point. Jurors want to see plaintiffs who are trying to get better and want to reward a plaintiff for having a positive attitude as well as those who attempt to do everything necessary to get back to normal. On the other hand, if a plaintiff is seen in his attempts to get better but who is caught unprepared to explain the activity, the jury may think that the plaintiff is lying. Consequently, in such a case a jury will not want to award anything to the plaintiff. Clients need to be prepared for social media, private investigators, and allegations (even though untrue) of what acts they are claimed to be able to perform. Again, the best advice is to tell one's attorney the whole truth.

OTHER TYPES OF PERSONAL INJURY CASES

The subjects and types of personal injury cases run the gamut of activities in which people engage. As just one example, personal injury cases can involve boating rules and reg- ulations. For example, I once had a case where a sheriff deputy's boat violated several boating safety rules with the result that it collided with my client's boat, destroying the boat and injuring both my client and his girlfriend. Knowledge of those regulations and the hiring of an expert in marine safety was a key to that case.

Another typical personal injury case is what is generally referred to as a "dog bite" case. In many states, as in Michigan, the law enforces a strict liability standard for dog bite cases. In strict liability cases, the injured party does not have the burden of proving negligence or showing that the dog has bitten other people. Thus, if a dog bites a person, unless that person provoked the dog, the injured party almost always wins. On the other hand, if the injured party can show that the dog previously was involved in injuring other people, then the amount of damages claimed by the plaintiff can be enhanced. In dog bite cases, attorneys obtain all records from the animal control division of the local jurisdiction as well as statements from neighbors who may be well aware of the dog's vicious tendencies. Dog bite victims often suffer significant physical and emotional trauma including permanent scarring. Most homeowners' insurance policies do, however, cover dog bite cases.

As discussed above, experience in a variety of cases is key in choosing the proper attorney. As indicated above, proper use of experts is often essential in proving a successful personal injury case. Understanding how work is performed by potential defendants in any given case is important. If one understands the intricacies of a particular manufacturing process, the procedures involved in medical treatment, or the federal regulations necessary to be satisfied from a safety point of view (such as in a products liability case), the injured party's attorney has an advantage. In reconstruction of accidents, it is important to obtain employee records, personnel files, contracts, subcontracts, correspondence, construction meeting minutes, traffic control plans, work sequencing plans, traffic control device plans, contract specifications (often published in book form by departments of transportation), work schedules, regulations regarding signage, etc. All these documents may show who is responsible for the injury and why they are responsible. For example, construction companies may sometimes perform work out of sequence resulting in a lack of proper caution signs that would otherwise be required to be placed in the construction zone. After reviewing the proper documents, attorneys can ascertain if the proper warning signs were used for the work being performed.

An understanding of construction contracts and subcontracts as well as specifications provides a basis for concluding what contractor or subcontractor was most responsible for the injury to a client. For example, if the subcontract shows that a certain subcontractor was solely responsible for signage on a job and there was a failure to place proper warning signs in accordance with universally recognized manuals, then the plaintiff's attorney can identify the primary target defendant. In cases such as these as well as other complex personal injury cases, attorneys must have experience and a basic understanding of the many variables involved in order to properly prosecute a case. Likewise, it is noted above, an attorney must also understand the importance of having experts such as traffic control engineers, design engineers, construction experts, biomechanics experts, accident reconstructionists, and toxicologists.

WHAT IS A "WRONGFUL DEATH" CASE?

"Wrongful death" is a phrase that refers to a personal injury case in which death has resulted from someone's negligent or reckless act. It is really a description of the result rather than the type of case. Wrongful death cases can result from motor vehicle accidents, construction accidents, medical malpractice, dog bites, falls, improperly designed goods or drugs, improperly manufactured goods or drugs, or similar events.

A cause of action for a wrongful death did not exist under the English common law, which became a part of the law of the United States when our Constitution was adopted. In the U.S., wrongful death claims are statutory causes of action. This means that each legislature in each state has at some time in its history passed a law known as the Wrongful Death Act. Understanding that wrongful death claims are fully defined by written statutes rather than by historical case law precedent (the "common law") helps people understand why they can only seek certain damages for wrongful death. For example, in the State of Michigan, several types of damages can be claimed under a wrongful death action:

- medical and hospital costs;
- funeral and burial expenses;
- conscious pain and suffering between the time of injury and the time of death;
- loss of financial support; and
- loss of society and companionship suffered by family members.

Other than funeral expenses which, although sometimes burdensome, usually pale in comparison to the other compensable damages defined by statute in a wrongful death case, all of these listed damages can be substantial. Pain and suffering from the time of the accident until the time of death, even if it is of a very short duration, can result in a substantial award of damages. For example, in cases of burn injuries resulting in death, eyewitness statements describing the victim screaming in pain until he died obviously demonstrates pain and suffering that would command an award of substantial damages. Likewise, loss of financial support is a significant factor in a wrongful death action. For example, if one assumes that the victim is 40 years old at the time of his death and would have been expected to work until age 65 to support his wife and children, one can calculate 25 years of lost financial support.

CAUSATION

Out of the 100 or more factors which must be taken into account in any personal injury case, perhaps the biggest factor is "causation"—what caused the accident. In the event of a fire, for example, attorneys must understand how fires start and how they spread. In the event of an automobile accident, attorneys must look at the laws governing motor vehicles. By reviewing, for example, speeding laws and the accident's location, attorneys and accident reconstruction experts can calculate the speed of the traveling car and how the accident occurred. While we all generally know how to operate a motor vehicle, sometimes we forget that which we learned when we first took driver's training. I often will pull out an old driver training manual during cross-examination of a defendant driver with the result that he often admits that he learned certain rules of the road as a teenager, but in this case failed to follow those very same rules causing the accident.

Unfortunately, there are many types of personal injury cases which cause death. For example, in one nursing home neg-ligence case I handled, the plaintiff died because nurses left him in his wheelchair wearing a vest that was supposed to support him in an upright position. The nurses had a birthday party for a co-worker and left him unattended in the general lounge area for 45 minutes while strapped into his wheelchair. In the meantime, the deceased had slumped down in his wheelchair and was strangled by the very vest that was supposed to support him. In another case, a piece of steel fell out of the back of a truck, bounced on the highway, and came through the windshield into my client's face, as her car followed the truck. People can die from all kinds of accidents, falling off ladders or falling through skylights. Often facts do seem stranger than fiction.

PERCENTAGE OF FAULT

In addition to investigating the cause of death, attorneys must also investigate all the various people who may have contributed to the death. In Michigan and in other states, statutes allocate fault among responsible persons based upon their percentage of fault. A percentage of fault can be allocated not only to the defendants but also to the plaintiff and even to non-parties. For example, even if a party cannot be made a defendant in a case (such as a party who previously settled with the plaintiff and was released by the plaintiff or a party such as a state agency which may be immune from suit by statute), that party may be considered as a "non-party at fault." A jury may be required to consider allocating percentage of fault to that non-party using 100% as a total for allocating fault among plaintiff, party defendants, and non-parties. Knowledge of causation and theories of varying degrees of fault must be explored by the attorney as part of his duty to properly represent his client.

Is it always clear who is at fault and who is not in a personal injury case? No. I often tell my clients that a case is very rarely totally black or totally white. It must often be looked at in varying shades of gray. As an attorney, my job is to perform the proper investigation, prepare for trial by performing proper discovery, taking depositions, obtaining the proper experts, doing proper analysis, looking at all the documents and facts, and then attempting to make my client's side of the case appear whiter (or less gray) while making the other side of the case appear more black and less white. This is done through hard work, experience, and applying skills and intellect to properly represent my client. For example, in a trucking accident case, the repair facility may not have repaired the brakes correctly, the truck driver may have been speeding, or the trucking company may have told the driver he had to make a certain deadline. Perhaps the brake manufacturing company made defective brakes or the subcontractor installed the brakes on the truck improperly or the truck manufacturer provided a defective product. Maybe there was a blind corner where the road commission should have cut down the vegetation so that motorists could have seen each other as they approached the intersection. A bar owner may have served a visibly impaired person who helped cause the accident along with the other driver. All of these parties and facts must be examined and investigated in great detail.

Sometimes attorneys must take into account that their client is also somewhat responsible for the accident. Most states now have comparative negligence statutes as I described above, whereby all parties responsible for the accident are assigned a percentage of fault, including the injured person. In the past, the "contributory negligence standard" stated that, if a plaintiff was found negligent by even one percent, he could not collect any damages. Since this was a fairly harsh rule, virtually all states have done away with it.

THE BOTTOM LINE

If people have questions, they should talk with an attorney so that they will not second guess themselves years later. In a consultation with an attorney, make sure that the attorney is someone whom you feel you can trust; someone who has your best interests at heart instead of his or her own. The attorney should be willing and able to explain all the various procedures involved in a personal injury claim. He or she should also keep his or her clients regularly informed and involved in the progress of the case. The easiest way for an attorney to do this is to provide the client with copies of all letters he or she sends, including letters to the opposing counsel, letters to doctors asking for records, copies of briefs and filings sent to the court, and anything else that can keep the client fully knowledgeable of what is happening in his or her case. After all, it is the client's case, not the attorney's case.

As an attorney, I like contingency fee cases because they allow me to pursue all avenues possible to win a case, even if I spend far too much time on the case to justify what might be the anticipated recovery. When working on an hourly basis, attorneys sometimes have to be careful to avoid spending too much time on minor issues because a client is paying on an hourly basis. Contingency fee cases allow the attorney to fully represent his client by spending the amount of time necessary to win the case at trial or to obtain a satisfactory settlement without a trial. I always prepare every case as if it were going to trial. That assumption usually helps guarantee that the trial will not be necessary and that a reasonable settlement can be achieved without a trial.

Confidence and trust are important factors for a client choosing an attorney. As a client, you will be sharing a lot of emotion and time over months or even years with your attorney. Whatever happens in your case will possibly affect you for the rest of your life. If you do not trust an attorney that you meet in an initial interview, go see another attorney. You need someone in whom you have complete confidence to represent your best interests. You need someone who will keep you updated on the progress of your case, who sends you copies of documents and letters so that you can review everything on your own. This will make you a better witness, as well as letting you know that your attorney is working for you and doing his or her best to get the recovery you deserve. As a client, you always deserve the best. An attorney's duty to give you his or her best, no matter what the ultimate outcome may be.

(This content should be used for informational purposes only. It does not create an attorney-client relationship with any reader and should not be construed as legal advice. If you need legal

advice, please contact an attorney in your community who can assess the specifics of your situation.)

Made in the USA
Middletown, DE
05 September 2020

18168136R00156